WOMEN AND MINSTRY

An Examination of Paul's Instructions to Timothy

by Phil Roberts

Tentmaker Publications
1997

TENTMAKER PUBLICATIONS
121 Hartshill Road, Hartshill, Stoke-on-Trent, ST4 7LU

TABLE OF CONTENTS

PREFACE

THIS study arose out of a series on the family. In considering the role of the wife reference was made to Paul's teaching in 1 Timothy and to the limitations that he places upon the woman in 2:11,12. In 2:15 Paul calls for women to find their true vocation primarily in childbearing, having stated in the preceding verses that women are to be excluded from the role of teaching men and exercising authority in the church. In our day the role of women in the church and society has become an issue of great importance and some contention. Given this, and with regard to the numerous objections now raised to the validity of applying Paul's words as they have been traditionally understood, I felt it merited a separate study. For many women the restriction apparently placed on their role by Paul is considered unacceptable and a fresh way of understanding the passage must be found.

> "A new hermeneutic on the Bible's teaching about women is beyond the length of this article, but it is vital that the issue is tackled not least because present confusions and contradictions about a woman's role in the church are hurting people and discouraging them from taking an active part in the Church." [1]

In the light of this I have consulted a number of authors from both sides of the debate and have sought to answer the objections to the traditional approach point by point.

---

1. Gill Smith, "Women in the Church," <u>BUZZ</u> (July 1986), p. 21. It is apparent that Gill Smith considers the answers arrived at by the normal methods of biblical exegesis unacceptable and desires to see the rules changed so that we can come up with new answers. It is significant to note that the motivation is not to achieve clarity but acceptability.

INTRODUCTORY CONSIDERATIONS

The reason for choosing 1 Timothy 2:9-15

In order to keep this study within limits I wish to restrict our discussion primarily to the words of Paul found in 1 Timothy 2:9-15. This portion has been chosen as it is acknowledged by most writers to be the definitive passage on the subject. Though Paul addresses the issue in 1 Corinthians 11 and 14, these latter passages are not considered as clear as this.

> "...1 Timothy is the one passage which clearly addresses the subject of men and women in community leadership and is not also primarily concerned with directions for marriage and family." [2]

The significance of 1 Timothy

Paul wrote to Timothy as one who was to put matters in order in the church in Ephesus. His task involved confronting false teaching, safeguarding public worship and developing mature leadership. In 2 Timothy he is instructed to treat Paul's instructions as a "pattern of sound words". This terminology indicates that Paul viewed these letters, along with his other teaching, as a template or blueprint. A pattern of practice was to be established in the churches which was to be handed on to faithful men who would in turn teach others.

> *"And the things that you have heard from me among many witnesses, commit these to faithful men who will be able to teach others also."* (2 Tim. 2:2)

Paul was setting out a blueprint for church-life which was to be faithfully conveyed to future generations

---

2. Stephen B. Clark, Man and Woman in Christ (Servant Books, Ann Arbour, 1980): p. 191.

It is evident that the churches were united by a respect for universal practice as well as universal belief and Paul, as an apostle, was charged with laying this foundation.

> *"But if anyone seems to be contentious, we have no such custom, nor do the churches of God."* (1 Cor. 11:16)

> *"But as God has distributed to each one, as the Lord has called each one, so let him walk. And so I ordain in all the churches."* (1 Cor. 7:17)

Apostolic tradition was something to be held on to and not revised later when it suited the church.

> *"Therefore, brethren, stand fast and hold the traditions which you were taught, whether by word or by our epistle."* (2 Thess. 2:15)

The Corinthians were rebuked for their arrogance which led them to dismiss what was practised elsewhere.

> *"Or did the word of God come originally from you? Or was it you only that it reached? If anyone thinks himself to be a prophet or spiritual, let him acknowledge that the things which I write to you are the commandments of the Lord."* (1 Cor. 14:36,37)

To the Thessalonians he adds that they were to withdraw from those who departed from the pattern given.

> *"But we command you, brethren, in the name of our Lord Jesus Christ, that you withdraw from every brother who walks disorderly and not according to the tradition which he received from us."* (2 Thess. 3:6)

These verses help establish the background to Paul's pastoral epistles to Timothy and Titus as well as granting us an insight into how Paul viewed the teaching he was imparting.

Here we have then Paul's directives concerning a well-ordered church. The key verses are in chapter 3.

> *"These things I write to you, though I hope to come to you shortly: but if I am delayed, I write so that you may know how you ought to conduct yourself in the house of God, which is the church of the living God, the pillar and ground of the truth."* (1 Tim. 3:14, 15)

"These things" may refer to everything in the epistle, but they at least refer to chapters 2 and 3 with which we are concerned.

Given the verses we have considered, it is quite astounding that Joyce Baldwin, an author of a number of commentaries and former principal of a theological college, can declare:

> "In matters of organisation and structure, local churches are free to adopt whatever pattern is appropriate for their circumstances. No blueprint is provided in the New Testament." [3]

The context of 1 Timothy 2:9-15

Paul's discussion of the woman's role comes before his consideration of the matter of church officers. Paul insists that a woman should learn in silence and not engage in teaching and exercising authority over men. Having begun the chapter with an exhortation to pray for all classes, including kings and those in authority, he continues by expressing the desire that the men pray. Some have questioned whether Paul is placing stress upon the way the men ought to pray rather than upon the fact that it is the <u>men</u> who are to pray in every place (in every place where the people of God meet as a community for worship). Fairburn translates the verse as follows, reflecting the emphasis which the Greek conveys:

> *"I wish, then, that prayer be made in every place by men, lifting up holy hands, without wrath and doubting."* [4]

It was considered befitting the role of men in the assembly to pray as this was in keeping with Old Testament tradition.

> "The passage perhaps has as its background the Jewish view that the men had the primary obligation for the community's worship and intercession." [5]

---

3. Joyce Baldwin, "The Role of Women in the Church", <u>The Role of Women</u>, (Inter-Varsity Press, 1984): p. 175.

4. Patrick Fairburn, <u>Pastoral Epistles</u> (T & T Clark, Edinburgh, 1874): p. 120.

5. Clark, footnote *, p. 194.

We should be cautious before making a universal negative from a positive, that is, deducing that the women must not pray publicly. To handle the positive command in such a manner would be to conclude that the men ought to dress immodestly! One thing that can be determined is that there is positive encouragement given here to the men, who should consequently take the lead in praying. Whether women can pray publicly must be answered by a resolution of references such as 1 Corinthians 14:34-35 and 11:2-16, which is beyond the scope of this study.

Turning now to the women, he exhorts them to an inner adorning which will be reflected in appropriate outward adornment. The parallel between this and the admonition to the men is clear, as both are concerned with a heart condition appropriate for the worship of God. The focus of the passage is on order and submission, not on adornment and quarrelling, but the latter are symptoms of disorder within.

> **Paul wants both men and women to have a heart-condition appropriate for the worship of God**

Why should Paul raise the issue of quarrelling for the men and adornment for the women? Obviously he believes these were areas of sin to which the people were prone. Given that one of his great concerns in writing to Timothy is to prevent the spread of false teaching, it is significant that he sees this teaching producing two fruits:

"As I urged you when I went into Macedonia — remain in Ephesus that you may charge some that they teach no other doctrine, nor give heed to fables and endless genealogies, which cause disputes rather than godly edification which is in faith." (1:3,4)

"But we know that the law is good if one uses it lawfully, knowing this; that the law is not made for a righteous person, but for the lawless and insubordinate,..." (1:8,9)

"If anyone teaches otherwise and does not consent to wholesome words, even the words of our Lord Jesus Christ, and to the doctrine which is

according to godliness, he is proud, knowing nothing, but is obsessed with <u>disputes and arguments</u> over words, from which come envy, <u>strife</u>, reviling, evil suspicions, <u>useless wranglings</u>..." (6:3-5)

"*Now godliness <u>with contentment</u> is great gain.*" (6:6)

The false teaching that Paul was combating tended to result in quarrelling in the church and produce unrest among those who were in a position of subordination — in chapter 6 it being those who were slaves and those who were poor. To prevent such evils troubling the church he establishes the priority of prayer from hearts free of rancour for the men and of a godly attitude of submission on the part of the women. This attitude of submission leads to a prohibition on women teaching and exercising authority as such activities would be inappropriate.

In order to consider the teaching in detail we shall look at each verse in turn, giving opportunity to those who claim that women should be granted the opportunity to teach to put their case and raise their objections.

PAUL'S INSTRUCTIONS ON WOMEN TEACHING

An attractive adornment

"...in like manner also, that the women adorn themselves in modest apparel, with propriety and moderation, not with braided hair or gold or pearls or costly clothing, but which is proper for women professing godliness, with good works." (2:9,10)

As we have seen, Paul is addressing the need of a godly disposition in both men and women. For the women this inner attitude will be evident outwardly in a life lived. Rather than ostentatious display achieved by fine clothing and jewellery, it will be achieved by good works which will speak loudly of the true sincerity of the woman in question. In this passage there is an evident parallel with Peter's words.

"Likewise you wives, be submissive to your own husbands, that even if some do not obey the word, they, without a word, may be won by the conduct of their wives, when they observe your chaste conduct accompanied by fear. Do not let your beauty be that outward adorning of arranging the hair, of wearing gold, or of putting on fine apparel; but let it be the hidden person of the heart, with the incorruptible ornament of a gentle and quiet spirit, which is very precious in the sight of God. For in this manner, in former times, the holy women of God also adorned themselves, being submissive to their own husbands, as Sarah obeyed Abraham, calling him lord, whose daughters you are if you do good and are not afraid with any terror." (1 Peter 3:1-6)

Peter is dealing with the relationship of men and women in marriage, whilst Paul is speaking of their different roles in the church. The similarity between the two passages is striking. Both emphasise a gentle and quiet spirit which is in submission, and both see this as having consequences which are evident outwardly.

Those who hold that Paul's teaching was peculiar to him, meant only for a specific situation, or revealing an unrenewed Jewish prejudice, do well to consider the conclusion of Clark.

"[The similarity] points to the fact that we are dealing with a standard teaching of the early church for women." [6]

An apostolic command

"Let a woman learn in silence with all submission. And I do not permit a woman to teach or to have authority over a man, but to be in silence." (1 Tim. 2:11-12)

This forms the core of Paul's teaching on this subject, whilst verses 9 and 10 are introductory and verses 13 and 14 are explanatory. The two statements support each other, the former being a positive command placed before the restriction.

• All women or just wives?

Some have doubted that Paul intended to restrict all women by these commands and propose that the word "woman" can be translated "wife". This is an example of interpretation by means of looking up a lexicon and assuming that any meaning of a word can be inserted for it in any place. This is not the case, as the context must determine which meaning is relevant. If Paul is referring to a wife in v. 11 then he must be referring to wives in vv. 9 and 10, and husbands in v. 8. While we might agree to the possibility of wives in vv. 9 and 10, it appears clear that it is men as men who are encouraged to pray.

"…'women,' without the article = women as women; in verse 8 'the men' = these as distinguished from the women." [7]

---

6. Clark, p. 193.

7. R. C. H. Lenski, <u>The Interpretation of St. Paul's Epistles to the Colossians, to the Thessalonians, to Timothy, to Titus and to Philemon</u> (Augsburg, Minneapolis, 1961): p. 558.

• Learning and not teaching, on account of ignorance?

The charge to "let a woman learn" has been taken as an indication that the problem in Ephesus was one of intellectual backwardness among the women. If so, then once this was corrected, the women would not be forbidden to teach.

> "It is no surprise Paul forbids women with no education or knowledge of the Torah to teach. With no written Scriptures around they would be prone to heresy and wrong ideas. But is this the case now with the 1944 Education Act and women in theology colleges?" [8]

A closely related argument for limiting the passage's relevance to Paul's day is propounded by William Barclay.

> "This is a passage which cannot be read out of its historical context. It springs entirely form the situation in which it was written. It is written against a double background." [9]

This background, he says, was both the Jewish and the Greek. Under the Jewish law of the day a woman was not accorded the rights of a legal person. She was a thing, entirely at the disposal of her husband, forbidden to learn the law, and having no part in the synagogue service. The Greek woman fared little better it seems. She led a confined life in her own quarters, accessible only by her husband, and may not even have been present at meals.

> "We must not read this passage as a barrier to all women's work and service within the church. We must read it in the light of its Jewish background, and in the light of the situation in a Greek city. And we must look for Paul's permanent views in the passage which tells us that the differences are wiped out, and that men and women, slaves and freemen, Jews and Gentiles are all eligible to serve Christ." [10]

We shall examine the appeal to oneness in Christ later, but for the

---

8. Smith, p. 23.

9. William Barclay quoted by Dorothy R. Pape, In Search of God's Ideal Woman (Inter-Varsity Press, Downers Grove, 1979): p. 157.

10. Ibid., p. 158.

present we must address the charge that Paul is simply meeting a condition which is no longer valid in the late 20th century in western society. This argument fails on a number of grounds.

(a) As we shall see, Paul gives as the justification for his command the order in creation (2:13) and not the supposed ignorance of the women in Ephesus.

(b) If there was a place in the ancient world where the women could not be considered ignorant, then Ephesus had a claim to being it. It was a city where women were more likely to be educated. Pagan women had influential positions in society.

(c) It was in Ephesus that Priscilla, with her husband Aquilla, had been used of God to correct Apollos and point him in the right direction.

(d) Lack of education in the Scriptures prevents men as well as women from teaching and exercising authority.

(e) He does not forbid all teaching by women, which would be the case if they were ignorant, but restricts it to specific spheres.

(f) The evident regard that he had for Timothy's mother and grandmother, as well as his many co-workers, does not accord well with the view that he held the women of that day to be ignorant.

"...when I call to remembrance the genuine faith that is in you, which dwelt first in your grandmother Lois and your mother Eunice, and I am persuaded is in you also." (2 Timothy 1:5)

"...and that from childhood you have known the Holy Scriptures, which are able to make you wise unto salvation..." (2 Timothy 3:15)

"...Paul frequently had women 'fellow-workers', commended women as representatives from their churches (Phoebe), recognised the abilities of women such as Priscilla, thought that women could learn and should be taught, and, most telling of all, made no reference whatsoever to the relatively ignorant, uneducated state of women in his day as a ground for his position." [11]

11. James B. Hurley, <u>Man & Woman in Biblical Perspective</u> (Inter-Varsity Press, Leicester, 1981): p. 203.

• <u>Paul restricted by his Jewish upbringing</u>?

Not only do many hold that Paul was simply addressing a specific need of his day, but some see evidence in these words of a Paul who was not fully free from his Jewish prejudices. The argument comes in two forms, one less radical than the other. Joyce Baldwin considers that Paul had to deal with a developing understanding among Jewish converts of what true, new covenant freedom entailed. Because of this he was held back by Jewish Christian sensitivities and was forced to restrain the believers in the exercise of their liberty. This argument draws on the letter sent out by the council at Jerusalem touching on such matters as abstaining from blood and meat that was strangled.

> "Christian freedom could not go beyond what was generally acceptable, with the result that concessions were made to Jewish Christians and their scruples, for instance at the Jerusalem conference (Acts 15). The conservatism of the Jerusalem church which Paul constantly needed to conciliate may well have extended in some respects the demands of the Torah and the Prophets." [12]

> "It is arguable that, just as the church has moved beyond the New Testament toleration of slavery to a recognition that Christian principles forbid slavery, so too we can with a good conscience accept a larger place for women in the ministry of the church than was possible in first-century society." [13]

Once more the answer to this position is found in the reasons that Paul produces to back up his case. No reference is made to any "Jewish sensitivity", and this must be read into the passage. If this is the case, then it is hard to see how Paul's words could provide "a pattern of sound words" to be "held fast" and committed to "faithful men who will be able to teach others also". Given what we know of Paul it is unthinkable that he would so restrict Christian freedom for half the church on account of the prejudices of the day. That on occasions he paid deference to local sensitivities is of course true, but where this is

12. Joyce Baldwin, "Women's ministry: a new look at the biblical texts", Lees, p. 159.

13. I Howard Marshall, "The Role of Women in the Church", Lees, p. 196

the case it is made clear and was never enshrined in the "pattern" that was to form the foundation for church practice and belief.

> **Who is more likely to be influenced by culture –**
> **an apostle of Christ, or today's Christian leader?**

But what if these words reveal something more sinister? What if we are dealing with a sub-Christian attitude in the apostle arising from his Jewish upbringing? That such a suggestion should be made by liberal theologians is not surprising given their view of Scripture, but that it is now countenanced by some professed evangelicals is remarkable. In particular, they see Paul's argument of female submission in 1 Corinthians 11 as originating in rabbinical theology.

"The rabbis thought that when Genesis spoke of the woman being formed from the man, this implied that she was under man; but 'derivation does not entail subordination.'" [14]

This quote from Joyce Baldwin has profound implications for our view of Scripture. If Paul's reasoning here was based on rabbinic prejudice, how can we consider his teaching as authoritative in other areas? She goes on to comment on Paul's reference to "the law" in 1 Corinthians 14:34, which she also believes shows rabbinic influence.

"The law of which Paul was speaking was almost certainly the oral teaching of his day. Not one of the Old Testament writers appears to have been aware of this law, and Jesus certainly makes no reference to it. Did the true meaning of Genesis 1-3 have to wait until late in Paul's ministry to be revealed to the world, even though its truth applied to half of humanity? The suggestion is too fantastic to take seriously. Yet this is what we are being asked to believe." [15]

Evidently Joyce Baldwin holds that we are not to take Paul as

---

14. Baldwin, Lees, p. 173 with quotation from Paul K. Jewett, <u>Man as Male and Female</u> (Eerdmans, Grand Rapids, 1975): p. 126.

15. Baldwin, Lees, pp. 156, 157.

authoritative unless we can find another biblical writer to support him. Where does this leave our doctrine of apostolic authority? In the next paragraph she seems to accuse Paul of imposing an alien social structure on believers.

"In the Bible we find certain social structures, but they are incidental to its main message. Its patriarchal organisation is not part of the gospel, to be imposed on all believers." [16]

Some are as blunt as J.B.Phillips who said:

"It was not until I realised afresh what the man [Paul] had actually achieved, and suffered, that I began to see that here was someone who was writing . . . by the inspiration of God himself. Sometimes you see the conflicts between the pharisaic spirit of the former Saul (who could write such grudging things about marriage and insist on the perennial submission of women) and the Spirit of God who inspired Paul to write in Christ there is neither Jew nor Greek . . . male nor female." [17]

But was Paul suffering from a divided personality? On what basis are we to determine whether the teaching in a particular passage is that of Paul the apostle or Saul the semi-pharisee? On what grounds do we hold that the Spirit of God was responsible for Galatians 3:28, whereas rabbinic tradition has left us 1 Timothy 2:10? The only conceivable answer to this would seem to be that we consider ourselves able from our elevated perspective to judge the higher morality of the one than the other. But why do we think that we know more of the purposes of God than Paul who was granted "surpassing revelations?" Which is more likely; that the apostle Paul, hand-picked by Christ, was a child of his age and deeply affected by it, or that we are?

• Total silence?

"Let a woman learn in silence with all submission. And I do not permit a woman to teach or to have authority over a man, but to be in silence." (1 Tim. 2:11-12)

---

16. Ibid., p. 157.
17. J. B. Phillips quoted by Pape, p. 168.

The word Paul employs is not the same as that in 1 Cor. 14:34, which is the common word for making no sound. Clark helps us to understand the import of the term used here.

> "In some passages of the New Testament (e.g. Acts 22:2), hesychia refers to a process of ceasing to make objections or ceasing to be contentious. The word 'quietness' in these passages, then, refers to a condition that would be characteristic of those who are taught and receive what is being said." [18]

> "The term does not necessarily mean refraining from all speech in public situations or in assemblies of the community, but it would mean refraining from speech that would be directive or involve teaching." [19]

One cannot on the strength of this verse demand that women say absolutely nothing in the assembly of the saints, but in saying this, one must not go to the equal extreme of reducing the term to irrelevance. It is sad to see the way that some commentators in their desire to escape the force of Paul's words attempt to argue that black is white. "In silence" is hardly an appropriate expression to describe the action of public teaching.

• Submission?

"Let a woman learn in silence with all submission." (1 Tim. 3:11)

This brings us to the heart of the debate. Is the woman to be subject to the man in God's economy? Some will grant that this is so in marriage. But what of the church where there is "neither male nor female?" Some evangelicals go as far today as to suggest that any thought of subordination is unbiblical:

> "Many Christians thus speak of a wife's being equal to her husband in personhood, but subordinate in function. However, this is just playing word games and is a contradiction in terms. Equality and subordination are contradictions." [20]

---

18. Clark, p. 195.   19. Ibid., p. 195.
20. Letha Scanzoni and Nancy Hardesty, All We're Meant to Be (Waco: Word Books, 1975): p. 110.

This radical view seems to ignore the very nature of the Trinity as revealed in the work of redemption. Our Saviour was truly subordinate to the Father in order to effect our salvation, but this in no way threatened His essential equality with the Father as the second person of the Godhead.

For others, the fact of the subordination of one human being to another can only be understood by reference to the fall.

> "...woman's subservience is a consequence of the fall into sin. But Christ died to reverse the deadly effects of Adam's fall, and in Christ there is to be mutual submission (Eph. 5:21). In short, Genesis 3:16, is not a verse on which a valid justification of male dominance can be based, any more that it would support the necessity of difficult and painful childbirth." [21]

Before we consider the reference to Ephesians 5:21, we should see that this line of reasoning does not serve to explain his use of submission but simply presents Paul as contradicting himself. As we now turn to Ephesians 5:21 we do indeed see an exhortation to submit to one another.

> "*...submitting to one another in the fear of God.*" (Eph. 5:21)

To understand this verse as Joyce Baldwin and others do, however, ignores the structure of the passage and leads to some strange conclusions. Verse 21 forms an introduction to the section 5:22-6:9. In this verse Paul establishes a principle that must govern our interpersonal relationships. In the subsequent verses he lists three examples; husbands and wives, parents and children, and masters and servants. Each relationship is based upon submission of one to another. What is not in mind is that in these relationships both parties submit. To claim that the husband is to submit to his wife as the wife submits to him would lead us to make a similar application in the other two examples. In that case parents are to submit to their children (6:1) and masters to their servants (6:5). Radical thoughts indeed! But, what is more, we would have to conclude that Christ is to submit to His church. No; just as He never calls us lord, so neither do parents submit to their

---

21. Baldwin, Lees, p. 165.

children and husbands their wives. To claim that the husband submits to the wife by taking her into consideration and having her needs upon his heart is to confuse loving leadership with obedient submission. Christ gave us the pattern of true servant leadership, but He acknowledged that He remained our Lord. His leadership pattern was not one found in the world, but neither was it void of authority and the requirement of submission.

In reading Baldwin's arguments one is led to the conclusion that any role involving total submission and dominion by another is bondage.

> "That there has been male domination cannot be denied, but the glorious news of the gospel is that the second Adam came to the rescue and delivered our race from every kind of bondage." [22]

> "…Christ's work of regeneration overrides the result of the fall and tends towards 'Paradise Regained.'" [23]

Christ did not consider his relationship to his Father as bondage and yet was there ever such an example of total submission to the will of another?

> *"Most assuredly, I say to you, the Son can do nothing of Himself, but what He sees the Father do; for whatever He does, the Son also does in like manner."* (John 5:19)

> *"For I have come down from heaven, not to do My own will, but the will of Him who sent Me."* (John 6:38)

The idea that submission is bondage arises more from mankind's desire to be free from the dominion of sin and "liberated" unto their own will (a "free will"), than to be liberated biblically into a total submission to God.

For Paul and the other biblical writers, submission is not bondage. It is possible because of faith, as Clark points out:

> "The passage [1 Peter 3] says that a wife's quietness and peacefulness are rooted in her acceptance of God's order for her life and a trust in him. The wife can be submissive because she

---

22. Ibid., pp. 174, 175.
23. Ibid., p. 156.

knows that God stands behind Christian order, and he cares for her, either through her husband or sometimes in spite of her husband." [24]

"People in modern society limit authority by controlling the scope of someone's authority, specifying what decisions a person in authority can make. The scripture writers rarely define or limit authority in such a way. For them, it is righteousness — obedience to the teaching and commands of the Lord who stands behind the head's commands — which limits authority and protects the subordinate." [25]

Such submission Clark believes extends to every area.

"...the phrase "in everything" [Eph 5:24] means that the wife is to be subordinate to her husband in every area of her life. No part of her life should be outside her relationship to her husband and outside of subordination to him." [26]

"Therefore, just as the church is subject to Christ, so let the wives be to their own husbands in everything." (Ephesians 5:24)

Though it encompasses obedience to commands, it goes beyond this.

"Subordination extends beyond obedience to commands to also include respectfulness and receptiveness to direction. 'Submissiveness' is probably the best English term in such contexts." [27]

It must be remembered that it is the wife who is to submit herself and not the husband who is to make her submit.

"...subordination has a practical aspect in that it creates a greater effectiveness in their working together as one. The subordination that Paul encourages is something that the wife must choose to do." [28]

That such a concept is deeply offensive to our "freedom" loving day is not surprising, but that our modern society is deeply offensive to God can also be little doubted.

---

24. Clark, pp. 92, 93.
26. Ibid., p. 83.
28. Ibid., pp. 81, 82.
25. Ibid., p. 82.
27. Ibid., p. 92.

- Contrary to equality in Christ?

> *"For you are all sons of God through faith in Jesus Christ. For as many of you as were baptised into Christ have put on Christ. There is neither Jew nor Greek, there is neither slave nor free, there is neither male nor female,; for you are all one in Christ Jesus. And if you are Christ's, then you are Abraham's seed, and heirs according to the promise."* (Gal. 3:26-29)

We have already seen the reliance that is placed in this text to support the arguments of those holding to women teaching. This may be considered their 'Magna Carta'. Here is the real spirit of the new covenant, we are told. Gone is the old subservience of the curse and now men and women are finally equal.

Before we go on, let me stress that this verse does declare the most amazing privileges and, yes, equality. No longer is race, station in life or sex, a barrier to experiencing God's blessings. With regard to men and women, both may now enter in by that living way beyond the veil; both are heirs of God and coheirs with Christ; both have every spiritual blessing in the heavenly realms in Christ. But does this passage teach that there is now no distinction at all made between men and women? Are all differences with respect to role done away with? Whilst some may say this is the case, most maintain that at least this passage establishes that there can be no longer a barrier to women entering the ministry and teaching and preaching.

> "It will take time to get women in potent ministries, but there is nothing a woman cannot do on grounds of her sex alone." [29]

> "Mary [Cotes] still has three years of training left but when she qualifies she does not expect any duties like teaching or eldership to be barred to her on the grounds of her sex. 'All Scripture must be interpreted in context and when we do this, we see there in no discrimination between men and women in ministry,' she says with conviction." [30]

Some claim that forbidding women to preach denies the great doctrine

---

29. Douglas McBain quoted in "Women in the Church", <u>BUZZ</u>, July 1986: p. 21.

30. Smith, p. 24.

of the priesthood of all believers which was re-established at the Reformation. They do so as they believe this entitles all to exercise a teaching ministry. Both the appeal to this doctrine and to Galatians 3 show a fundamental misunderstanding that becomes evident when we take the arguments a stage further.

If we examine now the concept of the priesthood of believers, it proves too much if it is held that on this basis we can all be teachers. If we are all priests then we should all be teachers. If it is a function of a spiritual priest to teach, then we should all be teaching. But this is not the case. "Are all teachers?", asks Paul, rhetorically in 1 Corinthians. We must recognise that this doctrine does not deal with ministry function in the body at all, but rather with the freedom each of us now has to approach God and offer to Him a sacrifice of thanksgiving and praise.

> "...according to the eternal purpose which He accomplished in Christ Jesus our Lord, in whom we have boldness and access with confidence through faith in Him." (Eph. 3:11-12)

> "Therefore by Him let us continually offer the sacrifice of praise to God, that is the fruit of our lips, giving thanks to His name." (Heb. 13:15)

Turning to Galatians 3, we perceive the same difficulty. This passages establishes that we are all one in Christ; in particular, that we are all sons. It focuses on the privileges of salvation which come to us in Christ, without respect to nationality, status or sex. Now, inherent in the argument that this justifies women teaching and exercising authority in the church, is the thought that eldership and call to teach are privileges which should be open to all. But we have now moved from considering privileges which are possessed by all, to privileges which it is held should be open to all. The passage is held to establish equal opportunities when, in fact, it teaches equal privileges. The right to preach and teach is not possessed by all but is granted to some by God in His providence. If sexual difference did not bar one from the teaching office, other factors would. There is obviously the question of gift which all do not possess, as well as the question of age. Paul says that an elder must not be a novice. But in Christ there are both young and old, children and fathers, and they are equally one in Christ and possess already all the privileges that are ours in Christ. The passage addresses the issue of equal standing not equal opportunity. There are many "inequalities" remaining for those in Christ. We are all different and intentionally made so. God distributes His gifts as He wills. This is brought out in 1 Corinthians 12:14-31, which significantly follows verses that are parallel in their thought to Galatians 3:28.

"For as the body is one and has many members, but all the members of that one body, being many are one body, so also is Christ. For by one Spirit we were all baptised into one body — whether Jews or Greeks, whether slaves or free — and have all been made to drink into one Spirit. For in fact the body is not one member but many. If the foot should say, 'Because I am not a hand, I am not of the body,' is it therefore not of the body? And if the ear should say, 'Because I am not an eye, I am not of the body,' is it therefore not of the body? If the whole body were an eye, where would be the hearing? If the whole were hearing, where would be the smelling? But now God has set the members, each one of them, in the body, just as He pleased. And if they were all one member, where would the body be? But now indeed there are many members, yet one body. And the eye cannot say to the hand, 'I have no need of you;' nor again the head to the feet, 'I have no need of you.' No, much rather, those members of the body which seem to be weaker are necessary. And those members of the body which we think to be less honourable, on these we bestow greater honour; and our unpresentable parts have greater modesty, but our presentable parts have no need. But God composed the body, having given greater honour to that part which lacks it, that there should be no schism in the body, but that the members should have the same care for one another. And if one member suffers, all the members suffer with it; or if one member is honoured, all the members rejoice with it. Now you are the body of Christ, and members individually. And God has appointed these in the church; first apostles, second prophets, third teachers, after that miracles, then gifts of healings, helps, administrations, varieties of tongues. Are all apostles? Are all prophets? Are all teachers? Are all workers of miracles? Do all have gifts of healings? Do all speak with tongues? Do all interpret? But earnestly desire the best gifts. And yet I show you a more excellent way." (1 Cor. 12:12-31)

> **Gal 3:28 proclaims equal privilieges enjoyed
> by all believers, not equal opportunities**

Any worldly concept of power and authority was far from Paul's mind. His view of the authoritative function of teaching and eldership was in the context of humble service as a study of the imagery of the church as a body in this passage shows. The misunderstanding arises when eldership, office and ministry are thought to involve status and thus threaten oneness in Christ. Just as Christ's submission to the Father as the Son-Servant did not threaten His equality with the Father and deny His essential deity, neither does the submission of a wife to her husband make her less than her husband.

It is to be feared that the reasoning I have just exposed commonly exhibits an underlying attitude which is much more serious. In reading the statements made by those who challenge the teaching of these verses, one frequently finds the view of authoritative teaching and preaching down-played. This is demonstrated in the modern desire to have someone "share" a word, rather than preach. It is to be questioned how much the desire to see the pulpit opened up to women is a desire to see true biblical authority strengthened, and how much it comes from the spirit of the age which is anti-authority. For many the goal does not appear to be an opening up of the ministry but rather a democratising and eventual overthrow of the ministry. In the end it seems to be a case of "Who are you to tell me what to do?"

• Paul or the Holy Spirit?

"And I do not permit a woman to teach or to have authority over a man, but to be in silence." (1 Tim. 3:12)

Are we dealing here with the will of Paul only? What if the Holy Spirit calls a woman to teach and preach? Are we to ignore the leading of the Spirit? Are there not clear examples of God's blessing resting upon women who have taught and preached?

These questions are of vital importance. For many there can be no higher court of appeal than experience:

"The ultimate proof is that God is calling women. To deny the authenticity of their call shows little trust in God's power to guide us." (my emphasis) [31]

But can a subjective, inner call, be accepted as of greater authority than the explicit word of an apostle? For many the answer is that here we have Paul's personal will, "I do not permit..." As we have already seen, however, Paul expressed himself as an apostle (cf. "The significance of 1 Timothy" on p. 7) and considered what he wrote as having the full authority of Christ (and this in a passage in which he states that women are "to keep silent in the church").

"If anyone thinks himself to be a prophet or spiritual, let him acknowledge that the things which I write to you are the commandments of the Lord." (1 Cor. 14:37)

Concerning the authority granted to his apostles, our Saviour says;

"And whoever will not receive you nor hear your words, when you depart from that house or city, shake off the dust from your feet. Assuredly, I say to you, it will be more tolerable for the land of Sodom and Gomorrah in the day of judgement than for that city! ...He who receives you receives Me, and he who receives Me receives Him who sent Me." (Matt. 10:14, 15,40)

These statements make it vital that we recognise the authority with which an apostle operated. To hear him is to hear Christ Himself.

"To oppose Jesus was to oppose God Himself. To refuse to follow Jesus was to refuse to follow God. Later in the New Testament when Jesus sent forth His unique apostles (those commissioned not by churches or congregations, but by Jesus Himself), when they preached, when they acted, to oppose them was to oppose Jesus Christ." (his emphasis) [32]

We might also consider other occasions when Paul uses similar language. When he terms the gospel "my gospel" are we to take it to

---

31. Smith, p. 24.

32. Leonard J. Coppes, Who Will Lead Us (Pilgrim Publishing, 1977), p. 70.

mean that he had a private gospel? In fact, the objection to Paul's teaching must lead to a rejection of Peter's.

> "It is saying that not only the apostle Paul but also the apostle Peter are wrong. In fact, it is saying that all the instruction we get on the subject of marriage relative to this point, and on woman in authority in the church, in the whole New Testament and even in the whole Bible, is wrong. Let that come into focus: According to this position, God has allowed His church, both in Old and New Testament days, and His apostles and writers, to communicate that which is in error and out of accord with His revealed will. And not only that: we must say also that Jesus made no attempt to correct this misunderstanding in the areas of marriage and the church. In fact by selecting twelve <u>men</u>, Jesus perpetuated this supposedly horrendous, male-chauvinist approach." [33]

But to consider now the other points. What do we make of the claims of the Spirit's leading and gifting of women to teach and the apparent blessing which rests upon their labours? Would God have so gifted them if he had not intended them to use these gifts in the church? Surely, we "must obey God rather than men," it is claimed. Would God employ and bless something that He states is against His revealed will? The surprising answer to this question must be, Yes! God does indeed employ agents of whom He disapproves. Consider the case recorded in Philippians.

> "But I want you to know, brethren, that the things which happened to me have actually turned out for the furtherance of the gospel, so that it has become evident to the whole palace guard, and to all the rest, that my chains are in Christ; and most of the brethren in the Lord, having become confident by my chains, are much more bold to speak the word without fear. Some indeed preach Christ even from envy and strife, and some also from good will: the former preach Christ from selfish ambition, not sincerely, supposing to add affliction to my chains.; but the latter out of love, knowing that I am appointed for the defence of the

---

33. George W. Knight III, <u>The Role Relationship of Men & Women: New Testament Teaching</u> (Moody Press, Chicago, 1985): pp. 44, 45.

gospel. What then? Only that in every way, whether in pretence or in truth, Christ is preached; and in this I rejoice, yes, and will rejoice." (Phil. 1:12-18)

"Two very simple truths, which no believer disputes, explode the whole force of this appeal to results. One is that a truly godly person may go wrong in one particular, and our heavenly Father, who is exceedingly forbearing, may withhold his displeasure from the misguided efforts of his child, through Christ's intercession, because, though misguided, he is his child. The other is, that it is one of God's clearest and most blessed prerogatives to bring good out of evil." [34]

Dabney goes on to make a further telling observation.

"If the rightfulness of actions is to be determined by their results, then it evidently to be their whole results. But who is competent to say whether the whole results of one of these pious disorders will be beneficial or mischievous? A zealous female converts or confirms several souls by her preaching. Grant it. But may she not, by this example, in the future introduce an amount of confusion, intrusion, strife, error and scandal which will greatly overweigh the first partial good? This question cannot be answered until time is ended, and it will require an omniscient mind to judge it. Thus it becomes perfectly clear that present seeming good results cannot ever be sufficient justification of conduct which violates the rule of the word. This is our only sure guide." [35]

The calling felt to be from the Spirit is to be checked against the Word. The two evidently do not conflict.

"Again, the true doctrine of vocation is that the man whom God has designed and qualified to preach learns his call through the word. The word is the instrument by which the Spirit teaches him, with prayer, that he is to preach." [36]

---

34. Robert Lewis Dabney, <u>Discussions of Robert Lewis Dabney Vol. 2</u> (Banner of Truth Trust, Edinburgh, 9182, reprint from 1891): p. 99.

35. Ibid., p. 99.   36. Ibid., p. 101.

An amiable zeal may cause a person to mistake a human impulse for the Spirit's vocation. What would we say, for instance, if a sincerely repentant polygamist felt he was called to preach?

The Scriptural call does not merely come through the candidate, but by the assembly and the latter are to test claims of the Spirit's leading.

> "When God endows a woman as he did Mrs Elizabeth Fry, it may be safely assumed that he has some wise end in view; he has some sphere in earth or heaven, in which her gifts will come into proper play. But surely it is far from reverent for the creature to decide, against God's word, that this sphere is the pulpit. His wisdom is better than man's. The sin involves the presumption of Uzzah. He was right in thinking that it would be a bad thing to have the sacred ark tumble into the dust, and in thinking that he had as much physical power to steady it and as much accidental proximity as any Levite of them all; but he was wrong in presuming to serve God in a way he had said he did not chose to be served. So when men lament the "unemployed spiritual power," which they suppose exists in many gifted females, as a dead loss to the church, they are reasoning with Uzzah; they are presumptuously setting the human wisdom above God's wisdom." [37]

Finally, in response to the assertion that many women are so evidently gifted to teach and able to exercise authority that it would be cruel and unjust to restrict their avenues of service, one need only consider the very varied and extensive spheres of responsibility given to the woman in the biblical passages, especially in Proverbs 31. Are not teaching and leadership skills involved in many of these areas? We must at all times be governed by the explicit commands of Scripture and not by expediency and pragmatism. The use of "I do not permit" is stronger than saying "I do not suggest." This is an apostolic ruling, not a suggestion, nor a personal whim.

---

37. Ibid., pp. 101, 102.

- Only authoritative teaching?

"And I do not permit a woman to teach or to have authority over a man, but to be in silence." (1 Tim. 2:12)

An attempt is made by some to limit the implications of Paul's words by restricting the term "teaching," leaving open the possibility of women speaking and sharing from the word. In order to see whether this approach has any validity we need to examine the meaning of the term Paul employs. Lenski reminds us that what is being spoken of is Bible teaching:

"Paul refers to teaching Scripture and not to imparting intellectual secular information to the mind. The public teacher of God's people does not only tell others what they need to know, but in the capacity of such a teacher he stands before his audience to rule and govern it with the Word." (my emphasis) [38]

Clark agrees with Lenski's point that teaching from the Bible is the method by which the people of God are ruled:

"The teacher did not just give his views. He laid out what he expected the student to accept." [39]

"In other words, the scripture views teaching primarily as a governing function, a function performed by elders, masters, and others with positions of government. In this context, the connection between teaching, exercising authority, and being subordinate can be seen more clearly." [40]

"...it is enough to note that the rule in 1 Timothy states clearly that men are to exercise governmental authority in the Christian community, and the kind of teaching discussed in the epistle is an expression of the exercise of that authority." [41]

When women are said to teach it is significant that a different term is employed.

"Perhaps it is significant that the passage which exhorts older women to 'teach' younger women (Titus 2:3 RSV) avoids the

---

38. Lenski, p. 564.   39. Clark, p. 196.
40. Ibid., pp. 196, 197.   41. Ibid., p. 201.

use of the word didaskein. This may indicate that the teaching of women by women, because it did not involve the older women or the deaconesses having authority over the younger wives, could not be considered 'teaching' in the sense that didaskein would have conveyed." [42]

It is to be observed that many who defend a woman's right to preach and teach also hold a lower view of these functions. Today there is a concerted attempt to undermine true preaching. In many churches one is asked to "share" not "preach." We are told that people will not be "preached to" today. Coupled with this is a rise in inductive Bible studies in which the believer determines for himself the meaning and application of a passage. Now, this is not to be despised, but its going hand-in-hand with other developments seems to point to a rejection of authority. How many of us listen to a sermon as God's speaking to us through his servant? The term "share" does not convey the idea that what is taught is to be obeyed, but rather that it is to be discussed. What Paul is speaking of in this passage is not a limited aspect of teaching which only elders could do, the rest being done by men and women as they wished, but rather he is describing the nature of true teaching in the church of God which is both authoritative and a means by which the church is governed. We have a long way to go to return to such a state of affairs as pertained in the early church, and taking note of the restrictions placed upon those who would teach and exercise authority is a very vital first step.

> **Teaching in the N.T. church was authoritative and a means by which the church was governed**

• <u>What of women prophets</u>?

If women are not to preach and teach, why then were women gifted as prophets? That women were granted this gift in both Old and New Testaments is evident and one mark of the new covenant is that "your

---

42. Ibid., p. 200.

sons and your daughters shall prophesy." It is important to note a distinction between the role of prophets and teachers.

"Women were prophets. The daughters of Philip and women at Corinth were prophets (Acts 21:9; 1 Cor 11:5). The role of a prophet, however, is not a formal institutional role. It is charismatic gift." [43]

In the passage we are considering, Paul, who was fully aware of women prophesying, forbids them to teach men. Rather than again assuming that he is contradicting himself, we must seek instead to understand the nature of N.T. prophecy.

Some, however, appeal to the case of Deborah as an example of God raising up a woman to govern men. Must not Paul's words be interpreted in the light of this? Dabney outlines the reason why the case of Deborah is irrelevant.

"When a few of that sex were employed as mouthpieces of God, it was in an office purely extraordinary, and in which they could adduce a supernatural attestation of their commission." [44]

"There can be no fair reasoning from the exception to the normal rule." [45]

"If any one bring forward, by way of objection, Deborah (Judges 4:4) and others of the same class, of whom we read that they were at one time appointed by the command of God to govern the people, the answer is easy. Extraordinary acts done by God do not overturn the ordinary rules of government, by which he intended that we should be bound....He who is above all law might do this; but, being a peculiar case, this is not opposed to the constant and ordinary system of government." [46]

To argue from the example of Deborah who was inspired, and establish a rule thereby, is as false as if we should argue from Elijah that anyone sufficiently moved by godly zeal may take upon himself the functions

---

43. James B. Hurley, "Women in Ministry", Lees, p. 129.

44. Dabney, p. 102.   45. Ibid., p. 96.

46. John Calvin quoted by John W. Robbins, <u>Scripture Twisting in the Seminaries</u> (Trinity Foundation, Jefferson, 1985): p. 55.

of a magistrate and condemn another to death, as Elijah did the prophets of Baal.

Despite the case of Deborah, it remains a fact that in the Old Testament no regular office was allowed a woman. This state of affairs appears to have been continued in the New Testament, with apostolic sanction. In reading some of the pro-women-teaching authors, one gains the distinct impression that the lack of females in ministry roles in the Old Testament is somehow accounted for by Jewish prejudice and chauvinism. The truth is, of course, that this state of affairs was due entirely to the explicit, revealed will of God. Whilst biblical theology recognises a development in revelation over the period covered by the Scriptures (cf. Hebrews 1:1-2), it also sees God's law as consistently holy and righteous. It is to be feared that some of these writers might have imbibed aspects of the popular concept of an evolutionary development in Old Testament religion from semi-pagan origins. As a result of this too stark a contrast is drawn with the New Testament revelation. We need to bear in mind that the Old Testament is not a body of myths, legends and semi-moral statutes, but a perfect (yet incomplete) revelation of the character and purposes of God.

> *"For what great nation is there that has God so near to it, as the LORD our God is to us, for whatever reason we may call upon Him? And what great nation is there that has such statutes and righteous judgements as are in all this law which I set before you this day?"* (Deut. 4:7, 8)

• What kind of authority?

> *"And I do not permit a woman to teach or to have authority over a man, but to be in silence."* (1 Tim. 2:12)

Much attention has been paid to the expression "to have authority." Did Paul mean by this to restrict all exercise of authority in the church to men? Does not the term imply that it is wrongful usurping of authority that is condemned, a view given some sanction by the Authorised Version? Here is what some of the writers say:

"In 1 Timothy the problem seems to be women who usurped

authority from others, teaching when they had no gift nor training. Perhaps one of the wealthier women thought her social position guaranteed her leadership post. Or perhaps the church was even meeting in the home of a woman who was bossy and domineering." [47]

"In the situation envisaged in 1 Timothy the women were particularly liable to be attracted by false teaching; some of them were refusing marriage and the rearing of children. In both situations [in 1 Timothy and 1 Corinthians] women may have been using their opportunities for teaching to vaunt themselves over the men. If these dangers had not been needed to be curbed, the practical implications of the basic principles might have been different." [48]

"The force of 1 Timothy 2:12 is to warn against the temptation to take part in ministry from fallen, sinful motives." [49]

A difficulty arises due to the fact that this is the sole use of this expression in the N.T. and it is not found in LXX (the Greek O.T.); but further studies of its use in secular literature of the period have clarified its meaning.

"Authentien means to have authority over someone....In no case did the word have the negative or pejorative overtone of 'domineer'." [50]

"Until recently there were only a few known uses of the verb and it was necessary to guess whether it meant 'exercise authority' or 'illegitimately exercise authority.' Further examples of its use have shown that it does not carry with it the connotation of illicit authority, nor does it carry the connotation of 'domineer' ('act imperiously' or 'be overbearing') as some translations and even lexicons have suggested. It simply means 'have authority over' or 'exercise authority over.'" [51]

47. Scanzoni & Hardesty, p. 71.
48. Marshall, Lees, p. 195.   49. Ibid., p. 154.
50. Knight, p. 18. Knight published a detailed survey of the use of the word in literature surrounding the N.T.
51. Hurley, p. 202.

Discounting these findings for the moment, let us consider which of the suggested alternative readings best fits the context. The following meanings have been proposed and are examined in Clark's valuable study.

> a. exercise authority?
> b. usurp authority?
> c. domineer?

a. would prevent all exercise of authority in the church over men by a woman.

b. may mean the same as (a), although it can mean that it is wrong for a woman to take authority in an improper way. If the latter is true, then a woman may exercise authority if appointed in the proper way. This would serve to condemn usurpers like Athaliah (2 Kings 11:1-3).

c. would prevent a woman exercising authority in an autocratic way.

These conclusions lead to two ways of viewing the passage:

> i.   prohibiting all exercise of authority over men by a woman.
> ii. prohibiting all wrongful exercise of authority over men by a woman.

There are a number of valid objections to the latter view. Firstly, the overall structure of the passage gives no hint that Paul has in mind only women who are wrongly handling authority. The passage is simply addressed to women, following an exhortation to men. Secondly, the terms "teach" and "exercise authority" are parallel.

"They are intentionally linked. Both are also parallel to subordination and quietness. The passage prohibits a woman taking a position where a man is subordinate to her. If the ruling concerned the unruly taking of authority, then the passage would be addressed to both men and women." [52]

"Paul's language not only qualifies teaching as an exercise of authority, but by means of the 'or' before 'to have authority' also extends his prohibition to other exercises of formal authority." [53]

---

52. Clark, p. 198.   53. Hurley, Lees, p. 131.

Finally, we must take into account the justification provided.

> "It is out of place because it is women who are doing it, not because women are doing it in the wrong way." [54]

Clearly, Paul holds it to be wrong to have a woman fulfilling a role which involves her teaching or exercising authority over men. There is one further comment worth making before we pass on and this concerns the areas of teaching open to women. We have already seen that women are able to teach children, and this may presumably today include the Sunday School as an extension of the family. We should be hesitant though before legitimising the practice of women teaching women in ladies meetings. This has become very common and often involves doctrinal instruction and Bible teaching on a wide range of subjects. For many women these meetings effectively become their "church," as they are frequently prevented from attending other meetings. We should note the areas of teaching to be undertaken by women in Titus.

> *"But as for you, speak the things which are proper for sound doctrine: that the older men be sober, reverent, temperate, sound in the faith, in love, in patience; the older women likewise, that they be reverent in behaviour, not slanderers, not given to much wine, teachers of good things — that they admonish the young women to love their husbands, to love their children, to be discreet, chaste, homemakers, good, obedient to their own husbands, that the Word of God may not be blasphemed."*
> (Titus 2:1-5)

There is no warrant here for the setting up of a church within a church run by the women. That women should not teach and exercise authority in the church follows from the nature of the woman's role in the home.

> "Church government must be consistent with the government of the home, for if a woman had headship in the church (the higher institution), of necessity she would have headship in the home." [55]

---

54. Clark, p. 198.

55. Bruce Waltke, "Shared Leadership or Male Headship", Christianity Today, October 3, 1986: p13-I.

"It follows that women are to conduct themselves in the church as they would in the family. This is one reason why the teaching office is withheld from women in the church. We argue from family to the church, not from the current practice in worldly society to the church. Women are to be submissive as in the family, but all their gifts and usefulness are to flourish in the church as in the family. We distinguish therefore between mothers, sisters and widows, or, as in Titus, between aged women and young women." [56]

"If the present prohibition is restricted to public teaching (as seems most probable) it accords perfectly with the 1 Corinthians passage." [57]

Before leaving this section, it is helpful to be reminded that these verses do not say all that is to be said on the subject of women's ministry, far from it, but they do contain an important restriction.

"The passage should be allowed its full weight in the area it addresses, but it should not be treated as a statement of everything one needs to know about men and women in community service." [58]

The appropriate reasons

"For Adam was formed first, then Eve. And Adam was not deceived, but the woman being deceived fell into transgression." (1 Tim. 2:13,14)

Paul advances two reasons to support his case for the restriction on women teaching:

> (1) Creation: its order
> (2) The entrance of sin: its avenue

---

56. Eluned Harrison, "The Minister's Wife," Paper presented to Evangelical Movement of Wales Theological Course, Bryntirion, no date.

57. Donald Guthrie, The Pastoral Epistles, Tyndale New Testament Commentaries, Gen. Editor: R. V. G. Tasker, p. 76.

58. Clark, p. 192.

Reason 1: The order of creation

"For Adam was formed first, then Eve." (1 Tim. 2:13)

This, by being placed first, is evidently considered the more important. Paul establishes his arguments on facts that universally affect the human race, not merely the culture of his day. This is found to be so on other occasions:

"For the man is not from woman, but woman from man. Nor was man created for the woman, but woman for the man." (1 Cor. 11:8,9)

Not only was Eve made after Adam, but for the sake of Adam. Rather than Paul's reason for appealing to creation being studied his views are either dismissed as a throw back to his rabbinic upbringing, or simply ridiculed as nonsense.

"Most theologians and many others are quite happy with the rabbinic teaching that because Adam was formed first he was therefore naturally superior to Eve. As McNally points out, we do not know if the first human being was solely male or hermaphrodite. But even if he were all male, creation was in ascending order, from creeping things, to animals, to man, to woman." [59]

"If being created first are to have precedence, then the animals are clearly our betters." [60]

"If the reasons given by Paul to Timothy for not letting women teach — that she was born after man and was deceived by Satan — were completely unknown before, then we would certainly assume that they were a revelation of God to Paul. If they were repeated elsewhere in Scripture, that would make a stronger case. But since they are a clear reference to Rabbinic teaching, it does seem possible the comment may be of no greater weight to us today than was Paul's quotation to Titus that 'The Cretans are always liars, evil beasts, slow bellies' (Titus 1:12-13) and that he should act accordingly. At least one commentator suggests that in the Greek the first words of 1 Timothy 3 ('This is a true saying')

---

59. Pape, p. 177.
60. Scanzoni & Hardesty, p. 28.

could belong equally to the end of chapter 2 and no one has found evidence of such saying about bishops. Chrysostom was also of that opinion." [61]

Some, like Marshall, seek to modify the impact of Paul's argument:

"The insistence in the passage on the prior place of the man, as indicated in the creation story, cannot be ignored; but it is surely the case that in the modern situation, where a woman's teaching does not call this relationship into question, it should be permissible for her to teach." [62]

Whilst maybe accepting Marshall's conclusion that women can teach in certain circumstances (i.e. other women as in Titus, and children), can the "modern situation" justify modifying a creation principle? As Hurley observes:

"If Paul did not base his conclusions on culturally relative grounds but rather on creational patterns, any suggestion that other conclusions than his should be reached must show why Paul's appeal to creation was relevant for the church of his day but not for the church in ours. We cannot dismiss Paul's teaching by refuting arguments which he did not advance." [63]

Paul's argument is not merely chronological but concerns derivation. Man was not made from the animals. Nor is man made from the dust of the ground as if from some living entity, as Jewett appears to hold; rather, he receives his breath from the living God.

The whole concept of an authority structure built into male-female relations by dint of creation is anathema to many modern writers. In order to explain its presence in human society it is attributed to the fall, the consequences of which Christ came to reverse. Later, we shall consider the fall in detail, but sufficient to say now that what is in view in Genesis 3 is not the curse of a subservient order but the curse of an ungodly disposition. By referring to the order of God's creative acts, Paul takes us to something predating the fall.

---

61. Pape, pp. 206, 207.
62. Marshall, Lees, p. 193.
63. Hurley, Lees, p. 137.

The consistency of male headship appears to be further borne out by recognising the following points:

(a) God gives Adam His word prior to the creation of Eve.

(b) Adam is given the responsibility of naming the animals and later his wife (firstly as "woman" in Gen. 2:23, and as "Eve" in Genesis 3:20). [64]

(c) God in cursing the pair addresses Adam before Eve, even though it was Eve who sinned first.

(d) Though committing sin after Eve, Adam, as head and representative of the human race, is held responsible for the fall.

"Therefore, as through one man's offence judgement came to all men, resulting in condemnation,...For by one man's sin disobedience, many were made sinners,..." (Romans 5:18,19)

If we may ignore or adapt as convenient these creative principles, then there seems no logical reason why marriage may not also be exchanged for some other social arrangement. Jesus though, as Paul, looks to the creation accounts for justification of what he is teaching.

"And He answered and said to them, 'Have you not read that He who made them at the beginning, "made them male and female," and said, "For this reason a man shall leave his father and mother and be joined to his wife, and the two shall become one flesh"? So then, you are no longer two but one flesh. Therefore what God has joined together, let not man separate.' But they said to Him, 'Why did Moses command to give a certificate of divorce, and to put her away?' He said to them, 'Moses, because of the hardness of your hearts, permitted you to divorce your wives, but from the beginning it was not so.'" (Matthew 19:4-8)

**The issue is authority and submission,
not superiority and inferiority**

---

64. The full significance of naming as an aspect of exercising authority is brought out by Hurley, pp. 210-213.

Now, it needs to be said that the creative order does not make man superior to woman. The issue is authority and submission, not superiority and inferiority, though too often these are equated in worldly thinking. Men need to repent of their wrong attitudes towards women and their treatment of them as inferior. Women are neither playthings nor slaves.

Reason 2: The avenue through which sin entered at the fall

> *"And Adam was not deceived, but the woman being deceived fell into transgression."* (1 Tim. 2:13,14)

Paul's second reason to justify his teaching is objected to even more strongly than his first. "What possible reason does he have for claiming this? Here is surely evidence of his adherence to rabbinic tradition as it is well known that they blamed Eve for the fall," so claim his detractors. But is Paul demeaning women when he says this concerning Eve?

What he claims is that Eve was *"deceived,"* or more literally, *"utterly deceived."* This was, in fact, Eve's claim:

> *"And the LORD God said to the woman, 'What is this you have done?'*
> *And the woman said, 'The serpent deceived me, and I ate.'"* (Gen. 3:13)

No such claim is made by the man concerning his sin. We do not know why Adam took of the fruit and ate. That it was an irrational, foolish act with dire consequences is of course true, but why he did it remains a mystery. Paul simply states that the man was not deceived, a fact which cannot be disproved from the information we have. All Adam says is:

> *"Then the man said, 'The woman whom You gave to be with me, she gave me of the tree, and I ate.'"* (Gen. 3:12)

Given Paul's assertion most look for justification and many find this in women being constitutionally more susceptible to deception. Some commentators (male!), especially of a past century, wax lyrical over the constitutional differences between men and women. [65] A modern writer puts the case as follows, though in the end decides that Paul writes as he does for other reasons.

---

65. Cf. Fairburn, p. 129.

"Shortly after 1 Timothy was written (perhaps at the very time it was being written), women took a prominent role in Gnostic sects, a more prominent role than the one they held in the leadership among orthodox Christians. Women were similarly prominent in the development of Montanism. A case can be made for the view that women can be found clustering around new spiritual movements, both good and bad, in greater numbers than men. In short, one could reasonably hold that women have been historically more open to spiritual influences than men, and that they have been less inclined than men to concern themselves with establishing good order and sound doctrine." [66]

As a consequence most writers from the pro-women-teaching position expend considerable effort establishing that women, far from being weaker and more prone to be mislead, actually make very capable leaders and reliable teachers. But to argue thus is not to answer Paul (who does not employ these arguments), but to refute the commentators who have wrongly concluded that this is the reason lying behind Paul's restriction.

"Paul's point is the divinely appointed relation between man and woman. In that relation each must keep his or her place. To point to the ability in leadership deflects the thought." [67]

Clark observes the modern tendency to look for empirical evidence to back up a claim.

"Many accept the account of Adam and Eve as a revelation, but are not inclined to argue from it as the basis of a practice or rule in human relationships unless they can see an empirical foundation." [68]

Let us recognise that Paul says *"the woman was deceived"* not "woman is deceivable." In any case, if the reason for the woman not being able to teach is due to her increased susceptibility to deception it makes a nonsense of her being allowed to teach children, who are less able to discern error than men — a point brought out by many writers.

---

66. Clark, p. 204.　　　　　　67. Lenski, p. 570.
68. Clark, p. 204.

What, then, is Paul's argument? It is simply that in the fall a role reversal occurred which played a significant part in the eventual outcome.

> "...both Adam and Eve had to violate not only the command of God not to eat but also their respective positions toward each other in order to effect the fall: Eve her position of subordination, Adam his headship: she gave him to eat and he did eat (Gen. 3:6,12)." [69]

> "'The woman whom Thou gavest to be with me,' was <u>his</u> confession to the Lord, 'she gave me of the tree, and I did eat' (Genesis 3:12). Yes, but God had given her, not for authority and rule, but for kindly ministrations; to be a helpmeet by his side, not a directress to control his judgement or determine for him the course of life....Adam showed that he had fallen from his true position, and ceased to rule, as he <u>should</u> have done, with God." [70]

Adam's fault was to allow himself to be led by his wife. We have no indication from the text that Adam was deceived as to what he was doing. He did it, an irrational act, in response to Eve giving him the fruit. Paul therefore addresses both issues in this passage; the need for the woman to submit, and the need for the man to lead.

Clark shows how the biblical mindset would view the account of the fall in a totally different way than we do today. This approach he terms the "typological mode of thought."

> "The typological mode of thought would assume that if the woman was deceived and not the man, then the scripture must be indicating something about the place of women. Otherwise, scripture would not have preserved that feature in the story. Eve is a type of 'woman' and the fact that she was deceived is a part of this portrayal." [71]

That this is in fact the way Scripture often leads us to view Old Testament narrative is seen in another of Paul's epistles.

---

69. Lenski, p. 568.   70. Fairburn, p. 130.
71. Clark, p. 204.

"Moreover, brethren, I do not want you to be unaware that our fathers were under the cloud, all passed through the sea, all were baptised into Moses in the cloud and in the sea, all ate the same spiritual food, and all drank the same spiritual drink. For they drank of that spiritual Rock that followed them, and that rock was Christ. But with most of them God was not well pleased, for their bodies were scattered in the wilderness. Now these things <u>became our examples, to the intent that we should not</u> lust after evil things as they also lusted. And do not be idolaters, as were some of them. As it is written, 'The people sat down to eat and drink, and rose up to play.' Nor let us commit sexual immorality, as some of them did, and in one day twenty-three thousand fell; nor let us tempt Christ, as some of them also tempted, and were destroyed by serpents; nor murmur, as some of them also murmured, and were destroyed by the destroyer. Now <u>all these things happened to them as examples, and they were written for our admonition</u>, on whom the ends of the ages have come." (1 Cor. 10:1-11)

That this is how we are to view this passage may be confirmed by comparing 1 Corinthians 14:34. There Paul makes reference to the "law".

"Let your women keep silence in the churches, for they are not permitted to speak; but they are to be submissive, as the law also says." (1 Cor. 14:34)

As already noted, the failure to find such a reference in the law of Moses has led some to hold that he is here referring to rabbinic tradition rather than Scripture (see quote on p. 14). But this need not be the case at all. There seems to be no reason to doubt that Paul held that God revealed His laws, not merely through direct revelation to Moses, but also in His actions. If events in the life of Israel can be considered as furnishing foundational principles binding upon the church, why not God's actions in creation? Paul may well be referring to a law enshrined in the very constitution of the universe. On other occasions he appeals to the order of nature to establish a point:

"For this reason God gave them up to vile passions. For even their women exchanged the natural use for what is <u>against nature</u>." (Rom. 1:26)

"Does not even nature itself teach you that if a man has long hair, it is a dishonour to him?" (1 Cor. 11:14)

"(...for when Gentiles, who do not have the law, by nature do the things contained in the law, these, although not having the law, are a law to themselves, who show the work of the law written in their hearts, their conscience also bearing witness, and between themselves their thoughts accusing or else excusing them)" (Rom. 2:14,15)

Hendriksen reinforces this point:

"Her full spiritual equality with men as a sharer in all the blessings of salvation (Gal 3:28: 'there can be no male and female') does not imply any basic change in her nature <u>as woman</u> or in the corresponding task which she <u>as a woman</u> is called upon to perform. Let a woman remain a woman! Anything else <u>Paul cannot permit</u>. Paul cannot permit it because <u>God's holy law</u> does not permit it (1 Cor 14:34). That holy law is his will as expressed in the Pentateuch, particularly in the story of woman's creation and of her fall (see esp. Gen. 2:18-25; 3:16)." (his emphasis) [72]

Paul draws our attention to a particular feature of the fall, that of the reversal of roles. This he maintains is highly significant. His point is no more than this. He does not conclude that Adam was any less guilty, in fact, quite the reverse. Eve was at least deceived, Adam could make no such claim! The point is not that it is better to be led by a deliberate rebel than by an innocent but deceived woman! The issue is that

"...Adam was the one appointed by God to exercise religious headship, and...he was the one prepared by God to do so." [73]

In the event of the fall we are to see that the roles played by the man and the woman were pivotal. The deception of the woman was the first step in the fall and occurred before any thought of a curse. Christ undoes the curse, not the basic order that was violated in Eve's action.

Recalling that one of Paul's major concerns in this epistle is the danger of false teaching, he is in effect saying, as Chrysostom said:

"...the woman taught once and ruined all." [74]

---

72. William Hendriksen, <u>New Testament Commentary; 1 & 2 Timothy and Titus</u> (Banner of Truth Trust, Edinburgh, 1960): p. 109.

73. Hurley, p. 216.

74. Chrysostom quoted in Pape, p. 156.

Here is the solemn warning against departing from God's order.

An appointed sphere of ministry

"Nevertheless she will be saved in childbearing if they continue in faith, love, and holiness, with self control." (1 Tim. 2:15)

This limitation on the woman's role is then followed by an indication of the area in which she will find true fulfilment. Paul concludes the section with a statement that the woman "will be saved through childbearing," an assertion which has led to various interpretations. What did Paul mean by this? Some have felt it refers back to the promise of the Messiah, the seed of the woman, but this is forced and alien to the line of thought. Susan Foh understands it this way:

"Undoubtedly, Paul means to encourage the woman after he has limited some of her activities. He may be suggesting that bearing and raising children is not demeaning to a woman, that motherhood is an honourable and significant profession if she continues in her faith in Christ. Paul is in favour of motherhood, but to assume that Paul is restricting the woman to the home is to conclude too much from this verse." [75]

Some have found Paul's change from the singular to the plural in verse 15 rather confusing. Lenski proffers the following explanation:

"'The woman' is certainly Eve, yet the use of 'the woman' in place of her personal name emphasises her sex so that in v. 15 Paul may continue with the generalisation 'she shall be saved,' which applies to any and every woman, and after that with the plural 'if they remain in faith,' etc." [76]

Summing up the teaching of this section, Mary Pride says:

"Paul has just finished giving Timothy instructions about how men should pray and how women who profess to worship God should dress. Next Paul said women should learn quietly and submissively, not be teachers in the church. The next logical

---

75. Susan Foh, <u>Women & the Word of God</u> (Presbyterian and Reformed, 1980): p. 128.
76. Lenski, p. 567.

question would be, 'Well then, what can woman do for God if they are not supposed to teach?' Paul says that by persevering in our God-given role — childbearing — with a godly attitude, we will be saved. 'Childbearing' sums up all our special biological and domestic functions. This is the exact same grammatical construction as Paul's advice to Timothy that Timothy should persevere in his life and doctrine, 'because if you do you will save both yourself and your hearers' (1 Tim. 4:16) Timothy's particular path to heavenly glory was his preaching and example. Ours in homeworking, all revolving around our role of childbearing. After reminding women that they too have an important role, Paul then feels free to go on and discuss the qualifications of elders and deacons, secure in the knowledge that he has not slighted women by simply excluding them from church office without telling them they have an equally vital job." [77]

Her comments here are very enlightening. The parallel between Paul's words to the women and his words to Timothy are worth pondering.

"Nevertheless she will be saved in childbearing if they continue in faith, love, and holiness, with self-control." (1 Tim. 2:15)

"Take heed to yourself and to your doctrine. Continue in them, for in doing this you will save both yourself and those who hear you." (1 Tim. 4:16)

James Hurley observes that the verb "save" in this context does not mean "save from sin," as this is not our work, but rather, "save from a perceived danger." In chapter 4:16 that danger is the false teaching which was creeping in (cf. 4:1ff). In the earlier passage the danger is the temptation to assume the man's role (with the risk of being deceived into error?). This will be avoided, says Paul, when the woman gives herself to her rightful calling.

"I would propose the possibility that he is thinking instead that Eve and women in general will be saved or kept safe from wrongly seizing men's roles by embracing a woman's role. This allows the text to be read as it stands and keeps it in line with the

77. Lenski, p. 567.

issue in hand....he is speaking generally of a woman's role when he speaks of childbirth, using a typical part to represent the whole." [78]

With all the talk of liberation present in the current debate we shall end this section with the comment of Eluned Harrison.

"It is the sphere of the family in which Christian women are to be mainly engaged. They are not to expect to be 'liberated' from this by the 'Gospel.'" [79]

---

78. Mary Pride, The Way Home: Beyond Feminism Back to Reality (Crossway Books, Westchester, 1985): pp. 41, 42.

79. Harrison, op. cit.

THE EFFECT OF THE FALL UPON THE SEXES

Due to the fact that writers from the pro-women-teaching position frequently regard the traditional role model as a result of the fall (see quote on p. 20), it is necessary that we examine just what the consequences of the fall were.

Many feel that the traditional approach institutionalises the effects of the fall instead of seeing them done away with in Christ.

> "God's anger at the Fall is directed at Satan — 'Cursed are you among livestock' — not Eve. To the man and the woman he makes statements about the way the Fall will affect them: 'Your desire will be for your husband and he will rule over you' he tells Eve. Adam is told that he will have to work for a living. These are not statements of God's will. His will for the sexes is found in Galatians 3:26 'In Christ there is neither male nor female'. The New Testament marks the watershed in the way Christians are to treat women in the Church and in society. In Christ all things are to be made new and there is no reason to suppose this does not include male/female relationships, <u>unless you believe woman was created to be in submission to man before the Fall</u>." (my emphasis) [80]

It is thus held that women under the new covenant enjoy a liberation from the subservient role not possible under the Law. But this reveals a fundamental misunderstanding of the effects of the Fall. A clearer understanding is gained from Hurley's treatment:

> "The curse upon the woman divides into two parts. The first concerns the childbearing, the second her relation with her husband. The commands of creation (Gen. 1:28) include a calling to multiply and fill the earth. Childbirth was therefore a part of the pre-fall pattern for humans. As a result of the fall this process

---

80. Smith, p. 22.

will become very painful (3:16). By the grace of God, however, the process will not fail and live children will be born." [81]

The Fall did not establish new relations but distorted existing ones: man's to the ground; woman's to childbearing; woman's to her husband. By the grace of God, though, these relations are not entirely destroyed but are still fruitful.

It is fascinating to see how each of the curses affects some element in the creation mandate given to mankind. The command to "be fruitful and multiply" is made more difficult by the woman experiencing pain in bringing forth children, whilst subduing the earth is now not just work but toil, accomplished with "the sweat of your face". When we come to the third aspect of the commission we see that exercising dominion is rendered far more difficult by a struggle within the marriage itself. [82] The wife's desire, due to sin, will be to usurp the man's position as head and consequently there will be an absence of willing compliance. Not only will the man need to assert his authority over the earth, but he will now find it challenged at home.

"Genesis 3, rather than being the basis of an argument for

---

81. Hurley, p. 218.

82. For an understanding of the words of the curse on Eve, one can consult with benefit Hurley, pp. 218, 219; or Foh, pp. 67-69. Both note that the identical Hebrew construction is found in Genesis 3:16 as Genesis 4:7. To quote Foh: "In addition to identical language, the proximity of Genesis 4:7 to Genesis 3:16 suggests that a similar grammatical construction would have similar meaning. As in Genesis 4:7, there is a struggle in Genesis 3:16 between the one who has the desire (wife) and the one who must/ should rule or master (husband). Cain did not win his battle with sin, and the victory of the husband is not necessarily assured by God in Genesis 3:16b. The 'curse' here describes the beginning of the battle of the sexes. After the fall, the husband no longer rules easily; he must fight for his headship. The woman's desire is to control her husband (to usurp his divinely appointed headship), and he must master her, if he can. Sin has corrupted both the willing submission of the wife and the loving headship of the husband. And so, the rule of love founded in paradise is replaced by struggle, tyranny, domination, and manipulation." (Foh, p. 69)

differences of role between men and women in the church, explains the sorry state of relationships between men and women in this fallen world." [83]

"The subordination of woman to man was intended from the beginning but now that the harmony of their mutual wills in God is destroyed this subordination becomes subjection." [84]

To say that Christ removes the curse of man's authority over the woman is to say that he also removes the curse of work, which is not the case. Work was not cursed, but the ground, rendering work onerous. What is removed in the case of the male-female relationship is that which threatens to destroy the peaceful cooperation of the two wills; the oppressive rule of the man, and the reluctance of the woman to submit. We thus find Ephesians 5 commanding each sex to do what they are least likely to do naturally.

83. Daphne Key, "Response to Joyce Baldwin and howard Marshall", Lees, pp. 198, 199.

84. F. Delitzsch, <u>Commentary on Genesis</u> (T & T Clark, 1888): p. 166.

THE CONCLUSIONS TO BE DRAWN FROM THIS STUDY

The clarity with which Paul expresses the role of women

One might legitimately ask how, if Paul did in fact intend to forbid women teaching and exercising authority in the church, he could have expressed himself with any more clarity. Could his statements have been more plain, or his arguments more cogent? It is not without significance that many pro-women-teaching writers abandon the attempt to prove that Paul taught otherwise and instead seek to establish that his words were valid solely for his day and culture.

In marked contrast to the clarity of the traditional understanding of this passage are the various contrary explanations. One finds repeatedly phrases such as "may not," "need not," "could be," "is possible that." One is reminded of the practice in engineering of calculating the limits of a structure given the worst possible scenario. For instance, a bridge may be designed to withstand every possible eventuality occurring simultaneously. The likelihood of this happening is in fact so remote as to be almost discounted, but it helps build in a safety factor. The various ways round Paul's teaching we have examined may, in the judgement of charity, for any one phrase or verse, be conceivable. But in order for a satisfactory, credible alternative explanation of the whole passage to be established, these less likely explanations must all be true in each particular, so well does Paul cover himself.

The principles of exegesis employed in the current debate

Interestingly, few pro-women-teaching writers are willing to state that they have proved their case, rather they seem satisfied to have raised enough doubts concerning the prohibition to make it unworkable.

"Theologian Mary Evans of London Bible College has begun a serious new look at what the Bible says about women in her book 'Women in the Bible'. She tackles some of the toughest passages of Scripture — and shows that the 'women may not teach' lobby has a long way to go before proving its case." [85]

We may not be able to answer every conceivable question which the passage raises, but there seems to be a distinct reluctance among many to accept any of the conclusions until all these possible questions can be answered. This does not show an honest approach to Scripture. Some commentators seem to delight in making the passage less clear and fall woefully short of the goal of true exposition. As most tacitly admit that the passage apparently forbids women to teach, on whose shoulders rests the burden of proof? It is surely for those who are proposing to introduce a new practice to establish beyond reasonable doubt that it is in accord with God's Word. Why is it that many sit on the fence allowing women to teach and preach until it is proved they must not? In fact the proof for the traditional position, as we have seen, is not wanting.

> **Responsible exposition uses clearer passages
> to establish the meaning of less clear ones**

The approach to the Scriptures we have observed being employed is one which uses doubtful passages to interpret clear ones. This is contrary to sound interpretation.

"The infallible rule of interpretation of scripture is the scripture itself; and therefore, when there is a question about the true and full sense of any scripture, (which is not manifold, but one) it must be searched and known by other places that speak more clearly." [86]

Having reversed this process, the explicit statements of scripture are ignored and doubt reigns in their place. The very method employed by so many of the writers consulted seems almost to pattern itself off

---

85. Smith, pp. 21, 22.
86. Westminster Confession of Faith.

the approach found in Genesis.

> *"Has God indeed said.......?...You will not surely die. For..."* (Gen. 3:1-4)

The extent to which orthodoxy is being undermined by this debate

The very prevalence of the view which I have examined and refuted is frightening. If, as I believe, in Paul's mind was the danger of false teaching, then the widespread disregard for God's order is having dire consequences. The presence of women in the pulpit and on the oversight is relatively new, being little over a century old, but the movement promoting it is making great progress today. Robert L. Dabney, writing in the 1879, could say:

> "In this day innovations march with rapid strides. The fantastic suggestion of yesterday, entertained only by a few fanatics, and then only mentioned by the sober to be ridiculed, is today the audacious reform, and will be tomorrow the recognised usage. . . A few years ago the public preaching of women was universally condemned among all conservative denominations of Christians, and, indeed, within their bounds, was totally unknown." [87]

We need to recognise the influence of the world. Rather than immediately see Paul as a man bound by the thinking of his time, we need to examine how much we are influenced by the world. It is not without significance that in this issue the church is not leading the world.

> "There are fads and fashions in theology, just as there are in ladies' apparel. It was not until feminism became fashionable that Reformed writers took a serious interest in the matter and began to test the limits of exegesis in order to accommodate the latest cultural fad." [88]

The problem with the teaching which forbids women to teach and exercise authority over men is not that it unclear but that it is unpalatable.

---

87. Dabney, p. 96.   88. Robbins, p. xii.

The extensive range of spiritual ministries open to women

The husband being head of the home does not prevent the wife from fully functioning according to her gifts, neither should it in the other areas of legitimate ministry, both within and outside of the church. We have had occasion in the course of this study to observe the number of times that Paul speaks of the Christian women of his day in the very highest terms. In so doing he indicates that he prizes their fellowship in the work of the gospel and his words demonstrate that the activities in which they were engaged were very varied. We must not get these verses in 1 Timothy with their restriction out of perspective. Yes, he does stand firm and close a particular avenue, but only after he has actively promoted women's ministry elsewhere.

Many draw a comparison between the attitude of Paul and our Saviour with regard to women. The Lord Jesus is claimed to elevated the status of women in a way revolutionary for His day. Paul, however, is seen as the repressed woman-hater. This is a caricature and does not bear close scrutiny. Where does Jesus depart from the principles expounded in these verses? Which of the many women with whom He was associated did He commission to preach and teach? How many women did He choose to include in the Twelve? [89]

Whilst placing stress on the role of the women in the home and family, Paul lays the way open for godly and gifted women to be used in many vital areas of ministry, just as his Master before him. Let us ensure that

---

89. When the apostles are spoken of, our attention is soon drawn to Junia, mentioned in Romans 16:7 who, with Andronicus, is said to be Paul's kinsman and his fellow prisoner, and "of note among the apostles". Junia, we are informed, is a woman's name. Indeed, the name Junia might be that of a woman, though there is significant doubt so as to make the matter far from conclusive, but what does "of note among the apostles" mean? It is unclear whether this means he/she was an apostle or merely known to the apostles. In addition, how is the term apostle used here? Does it refer to one like Paul and the Twelve, an apostle of Christ, or to an apostle or messenger of the churches such as Epaphroditus in Philippians 2:25 and those mentioned in 2 Corinthians 8:23. As this latter category of apostle did not necessarily involve preaching, teaching or ruling, but rather being commissioned to perform some task of service, then there is no reason to limit it to men.

we do the same and not be guilty of considering sisters in Christ simply as tea-makers. It is possible that the action of Priscilla and Aquilla speaking with Apollos was an example of the spiritual gift of helps in action. [90] How many of God's intercessors, personal workers, and carers are women? A large number to be sure, and invaluable. Are their talents wasted? Anyone who knows the challenge of any one of these ministries would have to say that the most gifted feels inadequate for the task. In all this, let us remind ourselves that God has an eye to faithfulness, not acclaim or status. Only on that great day when we stand before His throne will we see the true value of unseen and little valued ministries here. God knows and will reward!

The importance of the woman's role in the home and family

I wish to close on a positive note, as this is indeed the note with which Paul concludes this section in 1 Timothy. Paul would have us all appreciate the importance of the woman's role. Her God-ordained function as the man's helper and as the one entrusted with childbearing and house-management is vital to the fulfilling of the purposes of God. Without her aid the task becomes impossible. Though she is not asked to rule the church and teach and preach, she is granted extensive areas of authority and influence which prove to be strategic in the furtherance of God's kingdom. In regard to childbearing, it is she who generally has a determinative influence upon the next generation. Motherhood is to be held in very high regard therefore when viewed from a biblical perspective.

---

90. Charles Haddon Spurgeon, in a sermon on the character Help in John Bunyan's "Pilgrim's Progress", described what he believed this gift to be. In so doing he stresses that spiritual counsel is one aspect of helps. In this regard Bunyan's naming his character "Help" is consistent. Help was the man who drew Pilgrim out of the slough of despond and set him on the right path again, lie also drew attention to the stepping stones of promise placed across the slough. Spurgeon saw the vital necessity of having key individuals within his congregation who were on the look out for and able to help fellow believers who were struggling spiritually. This is a helpful corrective to the dismissive view that many have of this gift. His sermon is found in <u>Pictures From Pilgrim's Progress</u> (Pilgrim Publications, Pasadena, Texas, 1973): pp. 35-65.

"For most Israelite women the great events of their lives were birth, marriage, giving birth, and death. A woman who had given birth, especially to a son who could carry on the family name and inheritance, had a special place of honour. Without children she lamented her fate, and was sometimes scorned. The social activity of which women were most proud and for which they were sometimes most valued was the bearing of children. So much did both men and women value the production of offspring that both Abraham's and Jacob's wives offered their husbands their servant girls when they themselves had not borne children (Gen. 16; 30)." [91]

The issue we must face today is not how we may open up church leadership and the teaching office to women but rather how we may correct the very low view we have in society at large regarding the importance and high calling of motherhood and running a home. Far from seeing themselves as too gifted merely to be doing these "mundane" tasks, the women I have quoted should instead be echoing the words of the apostle Paul in another context when he exclaims, "who is sufficient for these things?"

"Twentieth-century cultural developments make the selection of childbearing as the part to represent the whole seem inappropriate or strange. Public opinion is increasingly against the bearing of children. Both men and women often look upon children as a problem and a burden. In some circles the bearing and raising of children is viewed as the prime means of reducing women to bondage. This sentiment is sometimes expressed in the remark 'keep 'em barefoot and pregnant'. It is easy to see that Paul's remarks here will be abrasive if received from such a perspective. We have already considered biblical attitudes toward childbearing. The bearing of children was a central element in the definition of womanhood and in the fulfilling of God's calling to mankind. The selfishness of our twentieth century, which does not want its enjoyment of pleasures undercut by the financial and personal obligations entailed in raising a family, was not common in the

---

91. Hurley, p. 42.

first century. In his day the bearing of children which Paul selected as a part to represent the whole of the high calling of women was a valued activity which women embraced with joy and with pride and for which they were deeply respected.

"On the interpretation which I am proposing, we may paraphrase Paul as saying that women in general (and most women in his day) will be kept safe from seizing men's roles by participating in marital life (symbolised by childbirth), which should be accompanied by other hallmarks of Christian character (faith, love and holiness with propriety) which will produce the adornment of good deeds for which he called in 2:10." [92]

---

92. Ibid., p. 223.

APPENDIX

A Response to
"The Role of Women in the Church" [93]
— A Presentation of the Alternative View
by Patrick Mitchell

I am indebted to the writer of *The Role of Women in the Church* (from here on referred to as "The Alternative View") for the clarity and graciousness of the document. It is most helpful to have the arguments clearly laid out and the study has brought additional informative material to the debate over whether a woman may teach and exercise authority in the church. Of particular value is the overview of the historical context of 1 and 2 Timothy, and the list of general conclusions found at the end.

To save wearying the reader, I will endeavour where possible to avoid repeating material already found in my original paper entitled, *"May Women Teach and Exercise Authority in the Church"*. In addition, I have decided to divide this response in to two parts of which the former is the more important, the latter serving as background material to the conclusions set forth earlier.

Section 1   A General Response to the Alternative View

Section 2   A Detailed Consideration of the Arguments Employed in the Alternative View

---

93. Patrick Mitchell, <u>The Role of Women in the Church: A Presentation of the Alternate View</u> (Unpublished paper, Tipperary, 1992)

SECTION 1
A GENERAL RESPONSE TO THE ALTERNATIVE VIEW

We are asked to believe by the Alternative View that the writer of 1 Timothy held the following beliefs:

i.   That the church in Ephesus faced a particular problem due to false teachers and that, as a consequence, the command that a woman should not teach and exercise authority did not necessarily apply elsewhere.

ii.   That the Genesis account contains no hint of a male-female hierarchy.

iii. That leadership comprised solely of males, lacking as it does the female input and point of view, is unbalanced and in conflict with the very purpose of Eve's creation.

iv.   That, rather than drawing principles from his letters to Timothy, the rest of Scripture must be appealed to on the issue of women teaching.

v.   That if women show evidence of possessing the necessary gifts and graces, there is no reason why they should not teach and exercise authority, even in an eldership capacity.

With these views he wrote:

> *I desire therefore that the men pray everywhere, lifting up holy hands, without wrath and doubting; in like manner also, that the women adorn themselves in modest apparel, with propriety and moderation, not with braided hair or gold or pearls or costly clothing, but, which is proper for women professing godliness, with good works. Let a woman learn in silence with all submission. And I do not permit a woman to teach or to have authority over a man, but to be in silence. For Adam was formed first, then Eve. And Adam was not deceived, but the woman being deceived, fell into transgression. Nevertheless she will be saved in childbearing if they continue in faith, love, and holiness, with self-control.* (1 Timothy 2:8-15)

My conviction is that the Traditional View best fits the available data and that the Alternative View does not do justice to the 1 Timothy passage and the remainder of Scripture. Whilst agreeing that some of Paul's writings are difficult to understand (and in this category I would include 1 Corinthians 11), I hold that 1 Timothy chapter 2 is not as difficult as is claimed. It is controversial, but not unclear in its central teaching.

1. The importance of the debate

The need for hesitancy in stating firm conclusions based on these verses in 2 Timothy is highlighted in the Alternative View. Stress is laid on the fact that this teaching does not form part of the core of the gospel and of the theology of salvation. On the basis of this a plea is given for tolerance and acceptance that genuine evangelicals may differ on this subject. I agree with the need for respect and accept the sincerity of true believers who hold opposing views on this and other issues. What is in question is not a matter of personal salvation.

The importance of the present discussion must not, however, be underestimated. As is observed, how we interpret Scripture is the issue that underlies much of the "Women in Ministry" debate. [94] But there is more here than a difference in approaches to interpretation. The Traditional Approach does not view the importance of the debate, as is suggested in the Alternative View, as bringing into question the authority of Scripture primarily. As evangelicals we are, by definition, committed to the final authority of Scripture. What the debate does raise is the issue of the sufficiency of Scripture. Does Scripture furnish sufficient details to enable us to know how to govern the church in a godly manner and understand clearly how the sexes are to function in their respective roles; or are we left to the use of our reason and dependent upon extra-biblical cultural information? The answer to this will indeed have implications for the authority of Scripture, as Scripture cannot be held to be authoritative for that which it does not address! This is not a new disagreement for the same issue separated the Anglicans in 17th century England from both their continental counterparts as well as the Puritans within their own ranks. If we state that a subject is left open in Scripture or not covered, we remove that subject from the realm of the binding authority of the Bible.

---

94. Ibid, p. 6.

2. Did Paul possess a blueprint?

The Bible does not provide "an absolute blueprint answer to every question" [95] we are informed. Few have ever claimed that it does. Further, I did not claim that the letters to Timothy of themselves provided such a blueprint, even on the issue of church government. To quote:

> "In 2 Timothy [Timothy] is instructed to treat Paul's instructions as a 'pattern of sound words'. This terminology indicates that Paul viewed these letters, **along with his other teaching**, as a template or blueprint. A pattern of practice was to be established in the churches which was to be handed on to faithful men who would in turn teach others." [96]

Paul, as an apostle charged with the task of establishing churches and setting matters in order, acted according to a revealed plan. He described himself as a *"wise master builder"* in 1 Corinthians 3:10, responsible for laying a foundation. Such a builder would work according to a plan. [97] Paul communicated that plan in letters, by verbal instruction, and by living example.

> *The things which you learned and received and heard and saw in me, these do, and the God of peace will be with you.* (Philippians 4:9)

> *. . . . in all things showing yourself to be a pattern of good works; in doctrine showing integrity, reverence, incorruptibility, sound speech that cannot be condemned, that one who is an opponent may be ashamed, having nothing evil to say of you.* (Titus 2:7-8)

The purpose of Paul's instructions to Timothy was to ensure correct conduct in the house of God. The statement is not qualified by "given the present situation", as is the case in 1 Corinthians 7:26. Yes, there were specific conditions in Ephesus to be corrected, but we have no textual evidence to show that Paul's remedies were merely temporary

---

95. Ibid., p. 2.

96. See p. 7.

97. It seems very doubtful that the God who revealed in such detail the measurements of the ark and the plan of the tabernacle would leave such important matters to human ingenuity.

or peculiar to the Ephesus. Neither are we informed that, given certain developments, the situation would be reversed. Paul's purpose in writing to Timothy is not to **lay out** a blueprint, but to **apply** a blueprint to a particular situation.

The argument which says, 'if Paul was laying down a blueprint he was not successful,' may be turned round. If in fact the Holy Spirit, the ultimate author of Scripture, did in fact intend women to teach and exercise oversight, he failed either to give an explicit command or a clear example. Instead he permitted a command forbidding them to do so in a key epistle to remain unqualified. We know what Paul said in a specific situation. If this is not a reflection of a divine blueprint, then we are left guessing what he might have said in another context. We cannot be sure.

3. How do we view Scripture?

The greatest concern I have concerning the Alternative View is that is fails to account for the nature of Scripture. The crucial passage in this regard is found on p. 20.

> "Paul is not addressing the church universal for all time, but a specific problem in Ephesus. It is the principle that we are concerned with, and that simply is the women in Ephesus, far from being domineering should be submissive and quiet. Paul's 'I am not permitting' (v. 12) lacks any sense of universal imperative for every situation for all time. Yes indeed he always sees his commands as an Apostle commissioned by God (Galatians 1:1) as authoritative, but as in verse 8, where he wants men to lift up holy hands in prayer, his words lack the universal imperative. People holding to the 'binding for all time view' must also be following Paul's command in verse 8, on every occasion of public worship."

In an earlier note Paul is said to be

> "writing with the purpose of changing behaviour in a specific situation". [98]

---

98. Alternative View, p. 16.

Great emphasis is laid on understanding the context of Paul's instructions to Timothy. In this regard, the historical data set forth in the Alternative View is most helpful in granting a deeper appreciation of this letter. However, what is meant by the statement, "Paul is not addressing the church universal for all time"? Is it saying that only when he is are we to follow his instructions? The question then arises, 'When did Paul <u>ever</u> address the church universal for all time?' Every single utterance of the apostle Paul is addressed to a specific situation with specific problems.

Scripture is not Scripture because it speaks to the universal church for all time. Though it is true that it does, it is not for this reason that it is accorded the status of Scripture. This is the claim of some charismatics seeking to defend verbally — inspired prophecies. They reason that the difference modern-day prophecy and Scripture (both of which claim to be God's words) lies in the fact that modern prophecy is only valid for a specific situation and not valid for all time. This is faulty theology. Paul gives us the clearest definition of Scripture's nature in 2 Timothy.

> *All Scripture is given by inspiration of God, and is profitable for doctrine, for reproof, for correction, for instruction in righteousness, that the man of God may be complete, thoroughly equipped for every good work.* (2 Timothy 3:16-17)

Scripture is valid for all time because it is God's very words, literally words "out-breathed" by Him. Of course we have to take into account the unique situation into which it was given but all **Scripture** *"is profitable for doctrine, reproof, instruction and training in righteousness."* Paul was instructing Timothy how to correct error and change the behaviour of the Ephesian Church, but change it to a <u>biblical norm</u>. If this instruction "lacks any sense of universal imperative" what are we to make of 1 Timothy 2:1-2?

> *Therefore I exhort first of all that supplications, prayers, intercessions, and giving of thanks be made for all men, for kings and all who are in authority, that we may lead a quiet and peaceable life in all godliness and reverence.*

When we come to 1 Timothy 2:8 and the command to the men, I hold that it is indeed universally binding. I have no question whatsoever as to whether it applies today. The only question is whether Paul is using a metaphor for prayer when he speaks of *"lifting up holy hands"*. [99] If it is proved that this is not the case then we ought to assume such a posture in prayer.

The vital issue to determine is, 'Upon what basis was Paul responding to the errors in conduct in Ephesus, and with what outcome in mind?' Given the problem of the false teachers, was he seeking to return the church to normality or introducing a merely temporary expedient? The teaching on submission in this portion is in full accord with that found in Ephesians 5:22-33; Titus 2:3-5 and 1 Peter 3:1-7, indicating that a general principle is indeed being applied to specific situation.

4. Is there a creation ordinance?

In the desire to see no creation ordinance certain facts are overlooked. It is true that in Genesis 1:26-30 mankind is given dominion and this includes men and women. But Genesis I needs to be understood in the light of Genesis 2. The two passages give two different, yet complementary, perspectives on creation. In Genesis 2, Adam is created by God (v. 7) and then placed in a garden with the task of tending and keeping it (v. 15). In verses 16 and 17 he is solemnly commanded not to eat from the tree of the knowledge of good and evil. All of this takes place before the creation of Eve to be his helper. There is no evidence that God then repeated his commands to Eve separately. In addition, there is an implied rebuke when God judges Adam:

> *Then to Adam He said, "Because you have heeded tile voice of your wife, and have eaten of tile tree of which I commanded you, saying . . . "* (Genesis 3:17)

---

99. Commentators are agreed that the posture of raising one's hands in prayer was a common practice in antiquity. Whether Paul is emphasising this posture here is open to question due to his use of the qualifying adjective "holy". In the Scriptures one is also enjoined to lift up one's heart, so the 'raising' may be seen as metaphorical.

> *Who may ascend into the hill of the LORD? Or who may stand in His holy place? He who has clean hands and a pure heart, who has not lifted up his soul to an idol, nor sworn deceitfully. (Psalm 24:4)*

As expounded in my original study, the argument is not that women are more likely to fall or are less able, but that the Fall took place when roles were reversed.

The Alternative View takes its starting point as Genesis 1:26-28 and seeks to establish that —

> "From this passage it is quite legitimate to see how both men and women are to use all their talents and gifts in a number of ways. Both sexes can be scientists, politicians, musicians, environmentalists, teachers and doctors. All that is required is the ability to do the job. Sadly then it is in the church, supposedly free from discrimination, where women are barred from certain jobs solely on the basis of their sex." [100]

> "Those who believe that Genesis 2 and 1 Timothy 2 teach some kind of creation ordinance are really stating something quite remarkable. To be consistent they must demand that all women, in all societies, in all ages are under the authority of men. This subordination is general since it is enshrined in creation itself. Women should <u>never</u> be above a man in any job or any structure totally <u>regardless</u> of the man's inability or the woman's ability. It is illogical to propose a 'creation ordinance' and then seek to apply it <u>only</u> to the church. All women leaders should be demoted, all women over men are breaking God's ideal." [101]

Here is indeed a strong challenge. What do the Scriptures say?

There are three spheres of authority established by God in the Scripture: the family, the church and the state. In the patriarchal period before the formation of the state, the family head (the man) acted as both the head of the home and the priest. C.f. Noah (Genesis 7:1; 8:15-22); Abraham (Genesis 12:1-8); Job (Job 1:1-5); etc. The nations arose out of the family or tribe. We need to take note of the one nation which God formed to be an example and a pattern, the laws of which were designed to call forth admiration from those around.

"Surely I have taught you statutes and judgments, just as the LORD

---

100. Alternative View, p. 21.

101. Ibid., p. 22.

*my God commanded me, that you should act according to them in the
land which you go to possess. Therefore be careful to observe them; for
this is your wisdom and your understanding in the sight of the peoples
who will hear all these statutes, and say, 'Surely this great nation is a
wise and understanding people.' For what great nation is there that
has God so near to it, as the LORD our God is to us, for whatever
reason we may call upon Him? And what great nation is there that has
such statutes and righteous judgments as are in all this law which I set
before you this day?"* (Deuteronomy 4:5-8)

There can be no question but that the society of ancient Israel was
patriarchal. Was this because it reflected the prevailing situation in the
pagan nations around, or because God so ordained it? If He ordained
it, did He do so merely as a punishment after the Fall? There is no
indication that the laws in their patriarchal aspect were a punishment,
actually quite the opposite. They were to be viewed as the statutes of a
wise and understanding people given them as a blessing.

*Israelites, to whom pertain the adoption, the glory, the covenants, the
giving of the law, the service of God, and the promises; . . .* (Rom. 10:4)

These laws were <u>righteous judgments</u>, and we should be careful before
claiming that they embodied prejudicial and unjust requirements. The
old covenant was temporary and unable by its inherent weaknesses to
make anything perfect or to endure for ever, but did this mean that it
enshrined in law fundamental inequities?

The laws of Israel ordained male headship in the home, male priesthood
in the worship, and male leadership in the nation. Women were
occasionally found in charismatic leadership positions (i.e. Deborah);
but these, by their very nature, were not to be taken as the norm. Hence,
women might be found as prophets, but not as priests.

Does the new covenant evidence a change in this regard? When we
examine our Saviour's choice of the apostles we find not one woman
among them. Was his leadership team "unbalanced and in conflict
with the very purpose for which Eve was created"? Lacking a female
input and point of view did it bring into question "the equality of the
sexes"? Was Jesus so bound by the traditions and culture of the day

that he could not break free on this fundamental point? Of all the individuals whom Christ befriended and worked with, have we even one example of a woman teaching and preaching? The Alternative View appears to hold that "women were naturally already involved in public worship and instruction" in the early church. [102] On turning to the Acts of the Apostles, can we find any evidence of this? Are we to conclude that the very **silence** of Scripture speaks louder than its commands? Like the gaping holes in the fossil record for the theory of evolution, the absence of clear examples presents a major problem for the Alternative View.

Not only is there an absence of explicit examples, but there is the lack of an definite command. The most the Alternative View can claim from 1 Timothy is that women were not to teach in Ephesus; it cannot state that Paul commands them to teach elsewhere.

5. The nature of authority and submission

The Alternate View states that

> "in all the texts on the husband/wife submission, the wife's submission is never forced but <u>voluntary</u> and is very much in the context of the husband's responsibility to love her as Christ loved the church   Just as the church responds to Christ's love, it is the husband's duty to love first, the wife gladly submitting in loving response." [103]

Firstly, it should be noted that the wife's submission is indeed voluntary but still <u>commanded</u> by God! He desires and expects willing compliance; but where is the Scriptural let-out clause for either sex? Neither command is said to be conditional on the other fulfilling their responsibility. The only conditional clause built in is that derived from the remainder of Scripture to the effect that the husband's wishes must fall within the bounds of legality, morality and God's will. That leaves a lot of room for unpleasant and inconvenient demands, especially when they come from an unbelieving husband. [104] These commands

---

102. Ibid., p. 17.   103. Ibid., p. 27.

104. There is **no excuse** for a husband being domineering or harsh. Such

are not just for wives of godly, Christ-like husbands; neither are they only for husbands of gracious and spiritual wives. Far from building in lots of exceptions, Scripture is explicit:

> *Therefore, just as the church is subject to Christ, so let the wives be to their own husbands in **everything.*** (Ephesians 5:24)

The absence of a let-out clause is also observable in the case of the authority of the state and that of parents. Paul did not write Romans 13:1-7 in the days of a benign and tolerant government.

The last section on authority again shows some imbalance. Apart from the prejudicial word "dominate", there are fundamental misunderstandings concerning authority and, in particular, that exercised by the Lord Jesus while on earth. There is necessary stress placed upon the nature of true authority being for service. A position of authority is held both for the glory of the God who ordains authority and the good of those for whom one is responsible. Selfishness should be an anathema in leadership. But the aspect of servant-hood can be so overplayed that the other aspects of true authority are lost. Though the Lord Jesus came to serve, not to be served, he did so as the servant of the Lord (cf. Isaiah 42; 44; 53; 61; etc.). An elder is a *"man of God"*, serving the Lord by caring for His people. He is never to lord it over God's people as though he owned them, for they are God's people. But this does not deny that he is set in real authority over them.

> *Remember those who rule over you, who have spoken the word of God to you, whose faith follow, considering the outcome of their conduct.* (Hebrews 13:7)

> *"Therefore take heed to yourselves and to all the flock, among whom the Holy Spirit has made you overseers, to shepherd the flock of God which he purchased with His own blood."* (Acts 20:28)

Paul had indeed become a slave for the gospel and suffered much for the sake of those he served, but he was no doormat. The "sufferings, beatings, humiliations, imprisonment, slander and hunger" came from the world, not the believers. If the believers had acted like this they

---

conduct is in direct contravention of God's explicit command and disobedience in this regard will be required of him on the day of judgement.

would not have been tolerated as Paul was quick to exercise his authority **for the sake of the church and good of the gospel.** In accord with our Saviour, Paul "commanded," "instructed," "ruled" and "directed," (cf. 1 Tim 1:3; 4:11; 5:9,11,17 etc.). By so emphasising one aspect we distort the truth as much as if we had omitted something. The loving headship of the husband does indeed consider the needs of his wife, but such concern is never termed "submitting" to his wife. It is the wife who is consistently said to submit to her husband, in all things.

In today's world where we see a widespread rejection of authority in the home, in the school and in society at large, any exercise of authority can appear harsh. Democracy, whilst encapsulating some biblical principles, is not itself a prominent concept in the Bible. We must not be surprised if the church, both leaders and people, find difficulty in embracing a biblical position.

6. Conclusion

The Alternative View does not succeed in establishing a credible alternative to the Traditional interpretation of 1 Timothy 2. In its attempt to do so, it erects and then destroys the "straw dog" of the domineering man and the subservient woman to which the Traditionalist is also opposed. The reasoning employed in the Alternative View exposes the degree to which the sufficiency of Scripture is brought into question. Whilst holding to the final authority of Scripture it raises doubts as to Scripture's adequacy to meet the church's needs in these vital areas. In seeking to demolish an explicit command it erects a theory supported neither by precept, nor example. The issue is indeed secondary with respect to personal salvation, but of great importance when considering the doctrine of the church.

> *These things I write to you, though I hope to come to you shortly; but if I am delayed, I write so that you may know how you ought to conduct yourself in the house of God, which is the church of the living God, the pillar and ground of the truth.* (1 Timothy 3:14-15)

SECTION 2
A DETAILED CONSIDERATION OF THE ARGUMENTS EMPLOYED IN THE ALTERNATIVE VIEW

INTRODUCTION

(a) Scripture speaking for itself

The Alternative View states that this disagreement does not endanger the truth of the gospel and should be viewed in the same category as views of church government and baptism. It is agreed that true believers may sincerely differ on these issues and respect must be accorded them. However, where evangelical believers sincerely disagree on the teaching of Scripture one may draw one of two conclusions:

a.   Scripture on that subject is unclear and open to all the various interpretations.

b.   All, or all but one, of the views are incorrect.

We must not fall into the trap of considering Scripture to be unclear just because believers disagree over interpretation. Incidently, Anglicans do not claim to find their form of church government in Scripture, but in early church history. [105] This view of developing church structures appears to be sanctioned by the Alternative View. [106] The question must then be asked, "At what point does development cease and corruption begin?"

It is not correct to claim that differences over church government and baptism are incidental to the truth of the gospel. A study of history reveals that the practice of infant baptism, if held to be the sole criteria for church membership, has resulted in the loss of a distinctive evangelical witness within a generation. In the area of church government, it is observable that certain forms of government may result in the purity of a gospel ministry being undermined with consequent loss of the gospel itself. [107] Whilst, therefore, the issue of

---

105. C.f. Bishop Lightfoot's Commentaries on the Pauline Epistles.

106. Alternative View, pp. 14 & 19.

107. An example of this is to be seen in the Methodist circuit system which

whether women may teach can be seen as distinct from the essential doctrines of the gospel, it may be highly significant when considering the long-term health of the church and the need to safeguard the gospel. If the Traditional View is correct and the warning given by Paul is indeed based on the precedent of Eve teaching Adam, then the issue is of the utmost importance. This is especially so when the situation is that of a pioneer church. If God has revealed His will in this matter, and let us for the moment assume He has, then it is presumption to expect His blessing when we ignore it.

I wish I could share the optimism of the Alternative View in believing that Christians are agreed on a fixed core of Christian theology and ethics. The doctrine of eternal punishment has recently become again a focus for widespread disagreement. Yet this has been held by evangelicals for centuries to be an essential doctrine of the faith. In the sphere of ethics, varying attitudes towards abortion divide even evangelicals. Further, clarity has not prevented many Bible students over the centuries failing to agree on the deity of Christ — not an issue between true believers, I hasten to add.

(b) The issue of women in the church

The observation is made that:

> "when we come to controversial topics such as 'women in the church' **we all want and expect** the Bible to say certain things one way or the other". [108] *(my emphasis)*

On what basis is this assessment made? Is it true that all are prejudiced when approaching this subject? That some are is true on their own confession. Mary Pride, from whom I quoted in my original paper, approached these verses from the perspective of a militant feminist and came away with another view! It is as unjust to claim that those holding the Alternative View are motivated by a feminist logic and a rebellious spirit as it is to say that the Traditional View is motivated by

enables one heterodox minister to infect a number of congregations. Failure to follow biblical guidelines can also result in unsuitable and even unbelieving candidates being accepted in eldership.

108. Alternative View, p. 3.

a desire for male domination. I have quoted others who have observed that the Church's preoccupation with this theme reflects a vigorous debate in the secular world at this time. I made the point that:

> "We need to recognise the influence of the world. Rather than immediately see Paul as a man bound by the thinking of his time, we need to examine how much we are influenced by the world. It is not without significance that in this issue the church is not leading the world." [109]

Many coming to the Bible are motivated simply by a desire for truth and conformity to God's standard (on both sides of the debate).

The Alternate View is marred by the use of prejudicial language. It is implied that the Traditional View holds that a woman's position involves "subservience",[110] that a male headship involves "domination",[111] and that being in submission implies "inferiority"[112] or "devalues" a person.[113] No writer from the Traditional View is quoted as holding these beliefs or using these words. All that is sought is "submission" and "headship" — found within the relationship of Christ and the Father (equals)[114] and exemplified in the relationship

---

109. See p. 55.

110. Cf. Alternative View, p. 22.

The Complete Oxford Dictionary gives the meanings of subservience as:
1. Being of use or service as an instrument or means: serving as a means to further an end, object, or purpose; serviceable.
2. Acting of serving in a subordinate capacity; subordinate, subject.
3. **Of persons, their actions, etc.: Slavishly submissive; truckling, obsequious.**

111. Cf. Alternative View, pp. 23, 29, 30.

The Complete Oxford Dictionary gives the meanings of domination as:
1. **The action of dominating; the exercise of ruling power; lordly rule, sway or control; ascendency.**
2. The territory under a rule.
3. The fourth of nine orders of angels in the Dionysian hierarchy.

112. Cf. Alternative View, p. 36.

113. Cf. Alternative View, pp. 39, 43.

114. Consider the following verses: John 5:17-19,30; 6:38; 8:28; 12:49-50.

between Christ and the Church. If fault can be found in the God-ordained way in which Christ relates to the Church, then the Traditional argument collapses.

INTERPRETATION

(a) Background

As this section concentrates almost exclusively on the Corinthian passages, it is peripheral to the debate over 1 Timothy. The choice of limiting discussion to 1 Timothy 2 was deliberate as it is agreed that the 1 Corinthians passages are less clear and positively bristle with exegetical difficulties. We are left in a degree of uncertainty as to the exact meaning of Paul's instruction to the Corinthians in the matter of a woman's role, but certain facts appear to be established.

i.   Any "equality" claimed for men and women must not be understood so as to deny that the woman was made for the man in a way that is not true the other way round.

   For man is not from woman, but woman from man. Nor was man created for the woman, but woman for the man. (1 Cor. 11:8-9)

ii.   Men and women are different in certain respects which affect public worship.

   For a man indeed ought not to cover his head, since he is the image and glory of God; but woman is the glory of man. (1 Corinthians 11:7)

iii. The passage omits to mention the functions of teaching and exercising authority in regard to women. Women are said to prophesy and pray, neither of which are explicitly forbidden by Paul in 1 Timothy. Prophecy was a function open to women under the old covenant as we see in the case of Anna, Luke 2:36, and examples of women prophets are found in Acts. The exhortation to the men to pray in 1 Timothy cannot logically be made to imply a universal prohibition on women praying.

Confusion over the exact requirements that Paul lays down must not lead us to ignore the underlying principles that he gives. The rule that states that the clear passage should be used to interpret the less clear remains the safest guide.

(b) 1 Timothy 2

As stated in Part 1, much helpful historical background is provided here and the particular situation which Timothy faced is well presented. The point at issue though, is whether Paul was merely reacting to a current problem by imposing unique remedies, or whether in keeping with his usual practice he seeks to return them to a biblical norm.

Most of the points raised in the exposition are dealt with in my original paper, but some further comments are called for.

When it is stated that

> "(2) Elders together are responsible for 'managing' or 'caring for' the church. But whatever that might have actually involved in Ephesus we just cannot know. Anything more is speculation."

Is this true? They were certainly to ensure that the flock were guarded from wolves without and self-seeking leadership within (Acts 20:28-31). They were responsible to ensure that all things were done decently and in order and for the edification of the whole as this was a universal requirement (1 Corinthians 14:26-40, esp. v.33.). They were to ensure that the instructions concerning the widows were carried out (1 Timothy 5:3-16). They were to watch over the souls of those committed to their charge (Hebrews 13:17; Acts 20:28). To multiply examples would be tedious. The point is that they were to **rule** (1 Timothy 5:17; cf. Hebrews 13:17). This was a function involving the exercise of pastoral authority.

(c) 1 Timothy 2:8-15 the text

The Alternative View proposes that Paul's command is rooted in the fact that the women of that day were ignorant and thus disqualified. Given Paul's extensive involvement with women co-workers (though not, I believe, in teaching and oversight), is it credible that the Ephesian women were peculiarly backward? Ephesus was a leading and sophisticated city of the empire. In addition, Paul gives no indication of when his instructions will end if they are merely temporary. The Alternative View observes:

> "Some writers make much of the fact that Paul is commanding a

woman to <u>learn</u> at all....Thus they should 'not yet' be teachers or in authority because they are not yet qualified to be in such a position.

"However this seems to be making much too much of Paul's words which rather seem to imply that women were naturally already involved in public worship and instruction." [115]

The "not yet" [116] desired by those writers is indeed absent from the text, but where are the words "which rather seem to imply that women were naturally already involved in ...instruction"? If their instruction in the home and of other women concerning the duties of godly ladies is referred to, we have no disagreement as all accept this role.

What evidence is there for the view that women were already commonly teaching elsewhere? As one examines the New Testament one cannot find a single example that contradicts Paul's instruction here. I. Howard Marshall draws attention to the example of Priscilla in Acts 18:26. The fact that Priscilla's name on this occasion [117] comes first has been taken to indicate that she led in the instruction of Apollos. Even if this was the case, it is unclear what direct relevance it has to the present debate. Both she and her husband instructed him privately, outside of a church gathering, in a context where no eldership function was in question.

In the matter of teaching, the Alternative View appears to propose a rather limited view of the subject matter. It is stated that:

"teaching in the N.T. is usually to do with instruction in Scripture and specifically that dealing with the Gospel of Salvation (see 2

---

115. Alternative View, p. 17.

116. The addition of words in a text to clarify the meaning is a dangerous practice and can result in twisting Scripture (2 Peter 3:16). One may see this abuse most clearly in the case of the Jehovah's Witnesses' New World Translation. In "translating" Colossians 1:16 they add the little word "other" twice, thus making Christ a created being. We need to deal with the text as we find it, not as we may wish we had found it.

117. For "Priscilla and Aquilla", see: Acts 18:18, 26; Rom. 16:3; 2 Tim 4:19. For "Aquilla and Priscilla", see: Acts 18:2 and 1 Cor 16:19.

Timothy 3:15). Any teaching that misled people on the doctrine of salvation (as in 1 Timothy and also Galatians) was always dealt with severely by Paul." [118]

Is teaching to be so limited? Paul's claim to the Ephesian elders was to have declared *"the whole counsel of God."* We must be careful in assessing what is important in what God declares. Whilst it is true that certain doctrines are of central importance to the issue of personal salvation and form the core of the gospel, nothing which God has revealed is to be treated lightly.

> *"The secret things belong to the LORD our God, but those things which are revealed belong to us and to our children forever, that we may do all the words of this law."* (Deuteronomy 29:29)

> *All Scripture is given by inspiration of God, and is profitable for doctrine, for reproof, for correction, for instruction in righteousness, that the man of God may be complete, thoroughly equipped for every good work.* (2 Timothy 3:16)

The aim of Scripture and thus of teaching is to equip for godliness of life in every area.

What did Paul's plan include? Rather than limiting himself to the essential doctrines of the person and work of Christ, Paul showed himself quite willing to legislate on a wide range of matters:

Relationships within marriage: Ephesians 5; Colossians 3:18-19.

Relationships within the family: Eph. 6; Col 3:20-21.

Relationship of servants to masters: Eph 6; Col 3:22-25; 1 Tim. 6:1-2; Titus 2:9-10.

Conduct becoming both sex and age: Titus 2:1.

In matters of church government he covered such issues as:

Church discipline: 1 Cor 5; 2 Thess. 3:6-15.

The exercise of the gifts in public worship: 1 Cor 14.

Collections for the saints: 1 Cor 16:1-2 (notice *"orders"*).

Subjects of public prayer: 1 Tim 2:1ff.

---

118. Alternative View, p. 18.

Qualifications for church officers: 1 Tim 3:1ff.

Treatment of widows: 1 Tim 5:3-16.

Payment of elders: 1 Tim 17-18.

In addition, certain practices were laid down and were common to the churches:

1 Corinthians 4:14-17; 7:17; 11:2ff, 16; 14:33; 1 Timothy 2:8.

Timothy is charged with *"instructing the brethren in these things"* (1 Tim. 4:6) and *"commanding and teaching these things"* (1 Tim. 4:11). On what basis are we to exclude from *"these things"* the commands in 1 Tim. 2?

In the reference to Adam and Eve, Paul does appear to hold that there are two distinct reasons for his exhortation.

For Adam was formed first, then Eve. **And** *Adam was not deceived, but the woman being deceived, fell into transgression.* (1 Tim. 2:13-14)

We have already noted how Paul finds meaning in the order of creation in his letter to Corinth:

For man is not from woman, but woman from man. Nor was man created for the woman, but woman for the man. (1 Cor. 11:8-9)

It would seem therefore that he is not merely "stating the facts of creation" but drawing a conclusion from those facts.

In the matter of dominion, we might indeed see that dominion is exercised jointly. But does this rule out the headship of the man? What is the situation with the second Adam? Our Saviour is destined to succeed where Adam failed and will have all things subject to Him (Hebrews 2:5-9). His bride, the church, will be joint-heir and reign together with him. Already, Paul declares, we are seated with him in the heavenly realms. Does this rule out any thought of submission and headship? If this analogy is thought illegitimate due to the fact that Christ is both human <u>and</u> divine, why is the analogy in Ephesians 5 allowable? The point is that there can be joint dominion and yet submission and headship.

In the Fall, the devil, the man and the woman were all cursed. In the case of the devil and the man the curse is clear, but disagreement exists over the woman's. The text reads as follows:

To the woman He said: "I will greatly multiply your sorrow and your conception; in pain you shall bring forth children; your desire shall be for your husband, and he shall rule over you." (Genesis 3:16)

The Alternative View sees two curses and a blessing here. The curses are the pain in childbirth and the domineering rule of the man. But what of the *"your desire for your husband"*? How is this to be understood? Many believe that it merely refers to the sexual attraction she will experience. Now, the Alternative View objects when the Traditionalist says that male rule was established before the Fall. They claim it is **introduced** here as part of the curse. But they can't have it both ways. If this is the case, and I am not saying it is necessarily, then logically *"your desire for your husband"* must be also be something **introduced** as part of the curse. Are we to conclude that Eve knew no sexual attraction before the Fall?

A more consistent understanding is to view all three parts of the sentence as aspects of the curse. In this case the desire was something inordinate and, as I have pointed out in the original study, is best understood by desire to control (cf. Genesis 4:7). The statement that *"he shall rule over you"* may well be descriptive of male domination and a domineering attitude. These have been all too evident in male-female relations since the Fall, but it is not the intention of the Traditionalist to defend "domineering" or the need for "subservience" in the woman. The desire has been to see authority exercised and submission practised in a God-honouring way, not in a sinful way. According to this understanding then, the gospel may relieve all three. The first, pain in child-birth, is relieved to a degree by technical advance due to common grace. God's saving grace in the man and the woman will turn domineering and subservience, the second and third, into the loving exercise of authority and godly submission, respectively. The result for the relationship will be increasing harmony. Both Peter's and Paul's instructions are in full accord with this line of interpretation. Women are to be submissive rather than seeking to control men, and men are to be loving in authority rather than harsh.

AUTHORITY

The understanding of authority is confused on a number of points. To say that all authority is from God and is "like the grace of God, it is given to whomsoever He chooses" is to confuse two distinct issues. The first is the position of authority, dealt with in Romans 13:1-7. God has ordained authorities and prescribed their various spheres. Christians are to respect the occupants of these positions and submit to the position according to the command of God. Only when these authorities go beyond their legitimate boundaries is disobedience sanctioned (cf. Acts 4:19-20). The second is the authority possessed by an individual apart from the office. This may be termed "charismatic" authority and is to be seen in the Saviour (Matthew 7:29) and in the prophets as a result of the Spirit coming upon them.

The authority we are debating is that exercising over the church and recognised by the church according to God's word. It depends upon gifting from God and grace in the heart. To give the examples of Moses, Gideon and Paul in this context is misleading as these were directly commissioned by God and never required to be appointed by men. The possibility exists for women to be granted charismatic authority and we see this in the realm of prophecy. Such authority involved both the prophecy and the prophet being tested. But when we turn to consider eldership authority it is not "charismatic" authority. God has not chosen to directly commission elders but has instructed the church to do so, giving them detailed guidelines so as not to be mislead.

Authority is indeed given for a purpose and limited, including the authority of the elder. An elder in a church must be circumspect in not overstepping the boundary dividing his authority from that of the head of a household. In addition, the church does not control the state and has no God-given authority to do so. It may address its rulers with the Word but is not charged with the rule of the civil government. Occasionally authorities come in conflict, but to propose a scenario where an elder is still under authority to his mother is silly. An elder is not to be someone still under his parents' authority. Paul's instructions speak of him as *"ruling his own house well"* (1 Timothy 3:4). Jesus, once he commenced his ministry, was no longer under his early parents' authority (cf. Matt 12:46-50).